ILLUMINATION
Essays on Democracy, Culture, Peace and Social Development in Nigeria

ILLUMINATION
Essays on Democracy, Culture, Peace and
Social Development in Nigeria

Udenta O. Udenta

KRAFT BOOKS LIMITED

Published by

Kraft Books Limited
6A Polytechnic Road, Sango, Ibadan
Box 22084, University of Ibadan Post Office
Ibadan, Oyo State, Nigeria
☎ +234 (0) 803 348 2474, +234 (0) 805 129 1191
E-mail: kraftbooks@yahoo.com
Website: www.kraftbookslimited.com

First published 2015

ISBN 978–978–918–222–0 (Paperback)
ISBN 978–978–918–284–8 (Hardback)

First printing, March 2015

Dedication

To all the members of the Circle of Illumination and Enlightenment: Amb Yusuf Mamman, Dr Umar Ardo, Tar Uko, Law Mefor, Dr Yima Sen, Dr Kelechi Akubueze, Dr Godwin Udibe, Sunny Agollor and Ikeogu Oke.

Acknowledgements

My first thanks go to the organizers of the various fora where most of these selected papers were presented for providing the platform for positive discourse on the place of democracy, development and peace practice in Nigeria. I will remain particularly grateful to **Klubb Harmon**y for not only organizing the Christmas 2007 retreat where the paper on **"The Threshold of Peace: Constructing an Mgbowo Elysium in a Time of Social and Cultural Change"** was presented but for also issuing the paper as a published booklet which was widely circulated. Engr. Emmanuel Akpa and Mr Laz Chukwukelu deserve to be mentioned specifically in this regard.

My thanks also go to my wife, **Vivian,** for her patience, love and understanding as I battled to put finishing touches to this and the other works that make up my 20-book publishing venture, and to my son, **Chidera,** who has to forgo hours of play with Daddy as I holed up in my study, sometimes to the early hours of the morning, researching and writing. At eleven, he is already beginning to understand the primacy of the intellect in the overall development of the human person.

I will forever remain grateful to the ideas I shared with **Ambassador F. O. Iheme,** and **Dr Kelechi Akubueze** which enriched the re-working and enriching of portions of some of these papers. Three of us not only share a passion for operatic and classical music (they both critiqued the paper on "The Phantom and his Opera" written soon after the death of the legendary tenor, Luciano Pavarotti) but also an uncommon insistence that only the power of social illumination through intellect, knowledge and critical discourse can the Nigerian State be redirected to fulfil its near infinite possibilities.

To my worthy friend, **Prince Ama Oriji,** who helped in no small way in my task of completing this and other creative tasks I set for myself through constant devotion and encouragement; to my secretary, **Felicia Abia, Blessing**... and **Lilian**... who typed the manuscript with due diligence; and to my clerk, **Idika A. Idika,** and research assistant, **Ogochukwu Obiefuna** for running various helpful errands as I prepared this and the other works, I say a million thank you for always being there for me.

Finally, to the champions of democracy, social justice, human rights, peace practice and cultural illumination in Nigeria and beyond, whose courage and vision continue to inspire me, and whose unceasing voices alert us to the dangers inherent in insipient social complacency and culture of silence as Nigeria navigates a critical pass from military dictatorship to a challenging Civil Democratic Governance, my urging is for the constancy of noble thought and nobler action till social justice reigns over the season of waste and unbelief.

Preface

The papers from where the chapters grew out were originally written between 2000 and 2013. With the exception of "The Nigerian Democratic Process: A Note", "The Phantom and His Opera" and "The Triumph of Immortality", the rest were presented at various democracy-building and conflict resolution platforms organized by both national and international institutions and agencies.

One common denominator of all the selected papers is that they contain, in an organic and interdependent manner and context, the key ingredients that reinforce the practice of democracy, the search for the correct path and strategy of national development and the awareness that human culture best endures when peace is given a free reign. While the idea of a unifying theme was easily settled by interlocking contextual affinities already alluded to, this was surely not so with regard to the choice of a title that could best capture this thematic coherence.

I first titled the collection "Epiphany: Essays on Democracy, Culture, Peace and Social Development". But on deeper reflection I came to the inescapable conclusion that while the thematic range of 'epiphany' could be highly expanded or extended to accommodate social discourses, yet, its trenchant rooting as a mystical-religious paradigm of divine revelation implies a tenuous nexus with and transition to a wider claim of social knowledge. I have, therefore, sought for social revelation elsewhere, and settled for "Illumination", another problematic choice, that yet captures the essential spirit of the effort: to use the power of reality, imagination and consciousness to extend the frontiers of understanding about the Nigerian condition, and to draw practical lessons from that condition for the realization, if not the outright affirmation, of the Nigerian possibility.

In the course of the years between 1986 and 2008, I have written and presented over a hundred and fifty papers at seminars, workshops, conferences, strategy meetings and capacity building sessions on themes consistent with the papers selected in this collection. I am in the process of finalizing work on these materials, and will issue them as soon as possible as a four-volume study to join this first volume. My objective intention in this effort is plain enough: to use the power of the intellect in nudging a society steeped in the mentality of instantaneous gratification akin to that of members of a 'Cargo Cult' about the necessity of enlightenment, critical reasoning and constant questing and striving as the only secure basis of social transformation and cultural growth.

My expectation is that the era will soon dawn when the measure of a person's worth is predicated on selfless labour, sacrifice and measurable contribution to the goals of national transformation and not the contemporary national buccaneering mindset, with the concomitant nauseating material advertisements, artifacts and accoutrements that presently reign unchallenged.

Fittingly, I draw inspiration in this regard from the timeless wisdom of Boris Pasternak in **Dr Dhrivago**. Pasternak's lament about the "world of impurity, of brazen, insolent vice; of rich men laughing or shrugging off the tears of the poor, the robbed, the insulted, the seduced; the reign of parasites whose only distinction was that they never troubled themselves about anything, never gave anything to the world and left nothing behind", holds well with regard to the social, cultural and spiritual maladies that have afflicted the Nigerian elite.

Udenta O. Udenta
Abuja, January, 2014

Contents

Dedication 5

Acknowledgements 6

Preface 8

Introduction 15

Chapter One
Between Legislative and Executive Governance:
Structure of Relationship and Management of
Conflict – A Reflection 23

Chapter Two
Forging Inter-Party Collaboration as Electoral
Violence Reduction Strategy 37

Chapter Three
Democracy, Governance, Conflict Resolution
and Peace-Building 51

Chapter Four
Democratization: Overcoming Obstacles to Free
and Fair Elections 62

Chapter Five
The Place of the Youth in Nigeria's Democratic
Consolidation 71

Chapter Six
The Nigerian Democratic Process:
A Note 84

Chapter Seven
Women and Conflict Management:
The Role of Leadership, Capacity Building and
Networking 94

Chapter Eight
Building the Nigeria of Our Dream:
The Role of Trade Unions, Civil Societies and Citizens 103

Chapter Nine
Traditional Rulers and Peace
Practice in Nigeria: Evolving a New
Paradigm of Engagement 124

Chapter Ten
Identifying, Managing and Mitigating Conflicts
Between Local Governments' Legislative and
Executive Branches in Nigeria 142

Chapter Eleven
On the Threshold of Peace and Harmony:
Constructing an Mgbowo Elysium in an Era
of Social and Cultural Change 151

Chapter Twelve
The Relevance of the Humanities in a Technology-
Driven World 166

Chapter Thirteen
The Phantom, His Opera and Cultural
Obscurantism in Nigeria: A Reflection 177

Chapter Fourteen
LP and MJ: The Triumph of Immortality 190

Afterword 204

Appendix
Six Essays on Armed Words 206

Recommended Books and Other Research Materials for Further Reading 233

Index 237

INTRODUCTION

Now, let's task our cognitive resources a bit and engage in a form of paradigmatic reasoning, a deconstructive analysis that establishes linkages between ideas and reality. Two challenges await us here: the seduction of mankind by the paradox of myth and ritual and their genetic sources or root, and embedded in this, the even more popular parable of the chicken and egg. Further down the primeval line will be encountered the dilemma, not of human dawning, but the problematic nature of mankind's encounter with the element of materiality and the force of transcendence. In essence, was the secularization of the universe a divine injunction incarnated by the first Transcendental Cause or was the spiritualization of mankind the logical extension of the frontiers of human reasoning, a journey of search that begins at the upper air, and later, encompasses in its extensive and expansive consciousness, the idea of a hereafter broken down in the ancient Grecian imagination, into the Elysian Fields, the Valley of Oblivion and the Internal Regions?

This specific reference to Greek mythic cosmological structure with all the metaphysical, autochthonous, anthropocentric and anthropomorphic nuances it carries is but a particularization of a universal cognitive consciousness in that my village of Mgbowo, not to mention other ethno-cultural or sub-cultural groups in Nigeria and Africa, has a fully developed mythic system that interrogates, understands, interprets and integrates the universe in organic form. The interplay of terrestrial and extra-terrestrial forces in a cyclical continuum, as against either axiological or dialectical relationship between things, is a common human heritage,

15

as a riddle or a puzzle that defies clear demarcation.

What is the relationship between this kind of esoteric quest to a collection of essays dealing with plain, 'easy to explain' subjects such as democracy, peace, culture and social development? Plenty. Many may not perceive it, but the struggle for the humanization of Nigeria is challenged by a faulty perceptual paradigm that fails to apprehend these subjects in, first, their causative capacity, and second, in their inter-connectedness and indissoluble inter-dependence. Let us pose a few of the questions: Is democracy the cause of peace or its effect? Or is peace the cause of social development? What about culture, which successfully hides its cause and effect propensity, given its limitless terms of reference, cognitive diffuseness, and its sometimes troublesome prodigality that flows out of the range of ideas and ideals it accommodates?

Is culture, therefore, the master of all social knowledge, the status of which determines the place and logic of democracy, peace and social development in a polity such as Nigeria? In interrogating the Nigerian condition, and in the search for national direction, an exercise that will be meaningless without democracy, peace and social development, I readily go for culture as the starting point, as the catalyst for change, which will herald other positive national values. And in placing culture first, I stress only but few things; the *weltaunschang* or the prevalent world-view, particularly of the elite, and the *Zeitgeist*; that is, the spirit of an age or the spirit that defines an age.

The tragedy of the Nigerian state, and the persistent difficulties and setbacks in constructing a wholesome national community lie in the distance between the "ideas in the margin" and the indolent statecraft that powers the system. This sense of national dissonance and disconnection that separates two tendencies: the intellectual strength and strategic capacity of private citizens, at home and in the Diaspora, and the anti-cultural, anti-intellectual mindset of the bulk of the elite, which rewards indolence, mediocrity, instant gratification, cargo-cult mentality and gross materialism must be bridged significantly for progress to be made in various national directions.

If the world view of the Nigerian elite is properly defined, the spirit of the contemporary Nigerian age becomes unfurled, and then we will but agree with Karl Marx in the *German Ideology* that the ideas of the ruling classes are the ruling ideas in any age, and the classes that control the means of material production also control the means of ideas generation, whether as social thesis or mental construct. Therein lies the power of culture as the pre-determinant of social reality, as the carrier of sacred wisdom on which democracy, peace and social development subsist.

From culture we encounter democracy – its highest social celebration, its solemn testament. What is democracy but dialogue, the interchange of ideas and assumptions with power and governance as the ultimate prize? For democracy to thrive as some of the essays in this collection establish, an organic social space must be constructed. What does this space accommodate? Precisely four elements; sovereign power and will of the people, freely expressed; instruments that establish the terms of democratic relationships; institutions that power the democratic system; and processes that shape democratic values in the context of human interaction. The specific details of these elements, and they are region, are in effect the various manifestations of democracy's spirit; its sense of being, its affirmation as a product of culture. In specific terms, if we must categorize them, we understand those elements as free, fair, credible and transparent elections and electoral processes; empowerment of human infrastructure and human security through good, accountable governance methods that honour integrity, probity, due process and transparency; free, unhindered contestation of ideas and viewpoints in a multi-party, plural political setting; and the politics of inclusiveness and mass participation in the formulation and execution of public policies.

Without a doubt, if the contemporary Nigerian world view, together with the spirit of our current age, is defined by the attenuation of the distance between human intellect and public performance whereby the former pushes up the cultural consciousness of the latter; and if the tenets and logic of democracy are honoured as indicated above, sustainable peace will characterize human relationship not only at the national level, but also in our various communities.

The relativity of peace can only be described in absolute terms. Even if the Nigerian age is defined by and possessive of the best spirit, and even if the instruments, institutions and processes of democracy are to function optimally, the nation will still experience conflict. The conventional conception of conflict as a universal phenomenon with inherent and enduring properties locates it only in the struggle between contradictory propositions, precepts and standpoints in faith, identity, resources and power.

Conflict never stands in opposition to peace as strange and paradoxical as this may appear. The notion of a permanent peace settlement (of a conflict) is as fallacious, absurd and untenable as it ever can be. Scholars and statesmen, policy formulators and policy executors, know this to their bones, and are therefore more comfortable with peace building and peace processes. So long as two or more people exist in Nigeria, conflict is bound to occur. What we hope for would be the right kind of conflict, as a catalyst or stimulus for change and rapid social transformation, and not the destructive type that tears a nation apart.

What is hoped also is to utilize the enormous space created by democracy for political and economic amelioration, and the building of a more tolerant and inclusive society, aside the specific apprehension of democracy itself as a paradigm for conflict reduction and transformation. In the pursuit of this, readers will encounter in some of the essays in this collection, key terms that define the peace and conflict spectrum: conflict sources and causes, methodological and research systems, conflict analysis, conflict indicators, triggers, regularity, tempo, dynamics, escalation, de-escalation, peace-building principles and elements(early warning signals and early responsive strategies, multi-track intervention processes, post-conflict reconstruction etc).These are some of the issues that state and non-state peace building actors must come to terms with in dealing with and responding to the various conflict situations thrown up in the Nigerian social, political, economic and cultural space.

Yet, not so readily advertised but perhaps more fundamental to the survival and future direction of the Nigerian State are other nuances of conflict that may defy neat categorization. There is the conflict between the purveyors of true humanistic, cultural and intellectual values who insist, as marginal as their ideas and views are today, that a modern Nigerian state can only be crafted through reason and logic, intellect and superior ability, competence and cultural exposure, and those others, currently in the majority, who are secure in their settled indolent, anti-cultural, low-intellectual mediocre mindset. For me, this is the greatest struggle of our time, the conflict between enlightenment, illumination and social epiphany in opposition to mindless mediocrity, obscurantism, incompetence and crass materialism that have for long seduced, ensnared and prodded an age of unreason and unbelief along the path of perdition and incoherence. Whether we like it or not, in the long run, it will be the end result of the conflict between these opposing forces: coherence and incoherence, intellect and obscurantism, culture and anti-culture and capacity and its lack that will determine the fate of the nation, and its authenticity as a vital social force in this century and beyond.

Social development, broadly conceived, and not narrowly understood, is the fourth plank on which these essays stand. It makes perfect sense to state that a positive national spirit, a thriving democratic ethos and a peaceful environment will naturally lead to the construction of a society that generates wealth and reduces poverty; in which human development index has positive attributes; in which human infrastructure and human security are its operating norms; and in which the heritage of the various national civilizations, serious literature, music and the arts and not their vulgarization and *mediocritization*, becomes the self-sustaining and self-perpetuating properties of all, and not merely the incidental past time of an infinitesimal percentage of the nation's elite.

In the search for a liberationist thematic, particularly the capacity of the intellectual to unfurl the banner of human freedom with the miracle of the written and spoken word, it is only proper that we summon the wisdom of Eduardo Galeano titled "In Defense of the Word" from his *Days and Nights of Love and War,* and quoted in his *Open Veins of Latin America,* to aid our quest:

> One writes out of a need to communicate with others, to denounce that which gives pain and to share that which gives happiness. One writes against one's solitude and against the solitude of others ...

> One writes, in reality, for the people whose luck or misfortune one identifies with – the hungry, the sleepless, the rebels, and the wretched of the earth ...

> Our effectiveness depends on our capacity to be audacious and astute, clear and appealing. I would hope that we can create a language more fearless and beautiful than that used by conformists to greet the twilight ...

> ... [Our writing] he continues, should be such that "does not propose to bury our dead, but to immortalize them, that refuses to stir the ashes but rather attempts to light the fire ... perhaps it may help to preserve for the generations to come ... The true name of all things ..."

Three essays in this collection have their own sense of uniqueness. The first is "Constructing an Mgbowo Elysium in an Era of Social Change", which, though dealing with the issue of peace and conflict, is particularized to a specific community, not ordinarily well-known across the length and breadth of our land. Yet, its struggles and triumphs, tragedies and self-exoneration, more than define the reality embedded in all of Nigeria's communities. Delivering that lecture was a kind of homecoming for me, a modest gift, criticism and satire all included, to an ancestral home that gave me life and inspiration.

The next is, "The Phantom, His Opera and Cultural Obscurantism in Nigeria", a journey of search for identity that locates squarely an operatic/cinematic cultural experience in the disjointed context of Nigeria's cultural non-being. The last is "LP and MJ: The Triumph of Immortality", a piece that started as a tribute to two geniuses and ended up being a problematic commentary on immortality — the quintessential idiom of all humanity, the struggle for self-preservation and self-perpetuation that many take for granted given the cargo cult-like haste with which the nation's grains gourds are daily wasted by the parasitic buccaneers in our midst.

Chapter

1

BETWEEN LEGISLATIVE AND EXECUTIVE
GOVERNANCE: STRUCTURE OF RELATION-
SHIP AND MANAGEMENT OF CONFLICT –
A REFLECTION

Introduction

When I was contacted to make a presentation at the historic
retreat for elected ANPP officials in the legislative and
executive branches of government, I accepted the challenge
with unqualified enthusiasm, convinced that two reasons
substantially informed that choice. Firstly, as a Director (as
I then was) in a well established agency charged with the
mandate of preventing, managing and resolving conflicts
in Nigeria and in the whole of Africa, I was deemed to be
possessive of adequate knowledge, skills and expertise
necessary in generating strategic positions and options in
addressing the problematic relationship between the
legislative and executive branches of government.

But probably, and most importantly, though a fact not
known to a large number of people here gathered, my
selection is a function of my close ties and bond to the party,

my involvement with its historical formation and institutional conditioning and the crucial role I played in crafting the All People's Party(APP) and Alliance for Democracy (AD) presidential alliance that threw up the Falae-Shinkafi presidential ticket in 1999. On paper, at least, I was the founding National Secretary of the grand alliance between the Committee of Fused Associations (CFA) and the Southern Leaders Forum (SLF) that metamorphosed into the original APP, the Secretary of the APP-AD Alliance Committee as well as the Secretary of the APP-AD Alliance Summit – the congregation of leaders and party elders who served as the conscience of the two parties.

Indeed, it was the break-up of that alliance, occasioned in part by presumably irreconcilable ideological differences, contrasting political philosophies and multiple contestations over the composition of the interim national executive committee, that threw up the two parties and led eventually to my emergence as the founding National Secretary of Alliance for Democracy (AD), and for the APP the emergence of Senator Ben Obi as its founding National Secretary before he was controversially replaced with Dr Josiah Odunna. Thus, the combination of my presumed knowledge of conflict resolution and my involvement with the party, by those who are familiar with its history and genetic sources, inevitably led to my selection to deliver this paper on a subject as challenging as the one before us.

My only introductory comment on peace-building here is that a theoretical knowledge of conflict, its dynamics, patterns and trends, and a sufficient intellectual grasp of the methodological and analytical contexts of engaging it are but mere preparations in our encounter with managing a real and existing conflict situation with all its complexes, contradictions, inscrutable quality and cogent, though sometimes, violent vitality. The same goes for all the structured learning about peace making processes, including but not limited to the anticipation and prediction of conflicts, examination of the behaviour of conflict indicators and the nature of conflict triggers, and the formulation of early warning and response strategies, including the institutionalization of systems and mechanisms that are sometimes piteously at odds, and tragically hapless in engaging conflict situations. Such accumulated learning should be seen as a mere guide in the articulation of conflict response and de-escalation options, and though it provides the scientific compass for productive engagement with conflicts it must have the reinforcing and self-regenerative capacity to be taught, schooled and tempered by existing conflict challenges.

In effect, while I am indeed a director in a peace-building institute and have learnt on the job both the requisites and practical necessities of engaging conflict scenarios, I will be deluding myself if I claim to possess the magic wand that would wish away the different layers, structures, and patterns of conflicts that develop among the managers of two great democratic institutions, with their peculiar histories and dispositions, personalities and motivations, in the context of an evolving democratic system with weak and problematic infrastructure and institutions. What I can hope to achieve is to set out a series of reflections on the key issues relating to the Nigerian democratic process; its structural and institutional overlay; and its mechanics and constitutive ingredients, especially as all these relate to the Legislative and Executive branches of government. In doing this, I will be interrogating a number of matters pertaining to the relationship between these two arms, the nature of conflicts underscored in such a relationship and some practical steps that could be helpful in attenuating them.

A final note is necessary here on the party, the ANPP. It must be admitted from the onset that the ANPP, like all other parties presently operating in the Nigerian social and political space, including the ruling PDP, is substantially challenged by a crisis of definition and philosophical and ideological direction. The historical context of the emergence of these parties, the content and character of the democratic transition, and the shape and form the democratic enterprise has taken in the past 9 years have stultified the organic growth of political parties as social formations with self-sustaining and self-perpetrating impulses and instincts; and have created a disconnect between the institutional design of mass participation in the democratic process and the necessity of elite political leadership. In this regard, we have a political process that has tailored political consciousness and objective political intention towards the acquisition of power in a system in which politics has become a means of material production over and above other social rationalizations that drive the engine of politics.

The ANPP has been grappling with these and other challenges since its fractured emergence. It has contended with and is still battling against internal implosion exacerbated by centrifugal forces worked into its being and existence, either as primary structures and forces, or as elements of fifth columnism with informal but potent access to its heart and soul. But most importantly, the ANPP is painfully contending with a multiplicity of ideological formations within its ranks, in a decisive, ongoing struggle between elements who still owe allegiance to its original, loosely conservative ideological moorings, and newer power brokers who canvass for a compact, rigidified ideological prerogative that is essentially exclusivist in nature given its self-ascribed moral purity and implacable enmity to any form of ideological compromise.

Where this struggle is headed and how it is ultimately resolved, only time can tell. But as leaders of the party, as you collectively reflect on this reality, thought should also be spared for these bigger challenges of identity, existence and being that have gripped the party, for in the resolution of the deep-seated institutional, organizational, ideological and philosophical contradictions embedded in the party may well lie the creative options and strategic roadmap essential for the resolution of the conflict that currently grips it.

I draw my imperative from a number of contexts. For a

start, a retreat of this nature substantiates the idea of democracy as a dialogue, as the interplay of ideas and viewpoints designed to strengthen its instruments, enable its institutions and infrastructure and consolidate its participatory processes. Through a series of reflections, the meaning and significance of democratic governance is deepened, and collectively we can begin to realize the implications of the trust, faith and confidence the people have reposed in their elected representatives.

The first context is the idea of democracy as a system of trust which guarantees the delivery of services. It is also democracy as constant dialogue, constant inter-change of varied perspectives, and constant refinement of viewpoints essential for the striking of compromises and the building of consensus. To this extent, therefore, this presentation is conceived as the sharing of practical thoughts and experiences necessary for the sustainable building of capacities essential for effective Legislative and Executive governance in an era of democratic transition.

However, the most important context of this presentation deals with its thematic trajectory: that is, the strategies, mechanisms and options readily available in resolving the periodic and systematic conflicts that emerge in the relationship between the legislative and executive branches of government. To properly handle a topic such as this, it will be necessary to interrogate a number of concepts central to its understanding. For example, we need to make clear and unequivocal statements on democracy as a system of relationships, the conflict potentials inherent in all democratic processes, an analysis of the fundamentals of legislative and executive governance, the concrete contexts of legislative and executive relationship and the disagreements and conflicts attending to them, and finally, the strategies and mechanisms of resolving such disagreements and conflicts. If we succeed in making eloquent and result-oriented statements on these issues, we would have advanced the practice of Nigerian democracy, and helped in enhancing its tenets, values and culture.

Democracy as a System of Relationships

Democracy is never an event, but a process-based system of relationships between various stake-holding groups who inhabit a determinate geo-political entity. It is primarily a relationship between all the people, the leaders, and the led, whose deliberate sovereign will make the idea of democratic governance a reality. Democracy is thus an act of freewill, an expression of freedom of choice and a deliberate acceptance of all its assets and liabilities, by all the people who participate in its processes and who share its promises and vision. Furthermore, democracy is also a form of binding relationship or executable social contract between the people and those they elect to represent them for the promotion of their interests, aspirations and expectations. By voluntarily surrendering their sovereignty to a set of individuals during free, fair, credible and periodic elections they expect, in return, the redemption of pledges and assurances on the basis of which this sovereignty was willingly surrendered in the first place.

However, democracy is yet again a system of relationship between the various institutions that regulate its practice and advance its cause. It is thus a system of relationship between the legislative and executive branches, which are established to perform certain constitutionally allocated functions, and a system of relationship between these branches and the judicial branch, which exist to regulate democratic conducts, adjudicate over conflicts and constitutional uncertainties and generally create the needful balance of interests that promote good governance.

In examining the system of relationships established under a democratic order, a number of things come to mind. This system cannot function properly, logically and coherently, unless key structures of democratic governance are put in place. Structurally speaking, therefore, the logic and coherence of democracy require the presence of democratic instruments, chief among which is the basic law or constitution that govern democratic practice. Other instruments include the acts of parliaments (Federal, State and Local Government) which must be consistent with and inherent in the constitution, and the various judicial pronouncements that settle, with clarity and finality, contentious issues in democratic governance.

The effectiveness or lack of some of these instruments, for example, the 1999 Constitution, determines to a great degree and extent the effectiveness of democratic practice observable in any historical epoch. Democracy also requires the existence of key institutions – the legislature, the executive and the judiciary. Again, the level of articulation of these institutions, their degree of maturity or advancement and their concrete social rootedness will also determine the degree to which the democratic order responds to the needs and interests of society and its people.

Finally, democracy is a process, and this may well be its most important element. The democratic process is a system of engagement, an inclusive and participatory dialogue in a complex social setting, involving stakeholders who have conflictual interests. The size of the "dialogue space", as it were; the freedom of choice available to the people within that space; and the degree of respect of contrary views in a diverse, plural and multi-party political framework determine the participatory nature of that democracy and the place of civil society structures in it.

Many commentators have already observed that democracy is a conflict resolution mechanism. This means that the aggregates of social conflicts find expression and ventilation in the context of democratic governance, and because opportunities abound for the interrogation of differences and the resolution of disputes using democratic instruments and institutions, democracy thus provides the best possible practice in enabling peace, harmony, culture of tolerance and respect of social and other diversities. Yet, democracy harbours enormous conflict potentials, which if not properly managed can weaken the democratic state, generate moments of uncertainties and induce stress and tension within the democratic system.

The reason for this is not far-fetched. Democracy opens up the space for the contestation of various interests, and if this process is not well-managed it can engender conflicts, some of which may be violent in nature. Some examples of this situation are to be seen in the militancy in the Niger Delta, especially in the past, and more recently the Boko Haram phenomenon, which assumed a wider dimension because of the space created by the democratic system; the initial extreme tension that attended the introduction of the Shariah Legal System in several states in Northern Nigeria; and certain local, state-wide legislations on appropriate dress code for men and women. Yet, the beauty of democracy, as evidenced in the past situation in the House of Representatives, whereby the Speaker and Deputy Speaker were compelled to resign from their positions[4] and the success of the mass Labour-Civil Society action over the increase in the prices of petroleum products and VAT[5], is its hidden or innate capacity to rise to this kind of challenge, generate its inherent conflict resolution mechanisms in addressing them, and achieve the right kind of balance that best secures consensus and guarantees compromise.

As would be presently seen, the relationship between the legislative and executive branches of government is not always cordial. This relationship is, often times, conflict-prone as a consequence of the interplay of personalities with differing degrees of ego, but most fundamentally because the framers and implementers of the constitution recognize that in exercising their various responsibilities and mandates, overlaps, and with that, conflicts are bound to occur.

The Fundamentals of Legislative Governance

Basically, as any good book on government tells us, the Legislature is the First Arm of Government, the bedrock of constitutional power and authority in a democratic state, and the highest expression of the collective sovereignty of the people. The Legislature, whether at the Federal, State or Local Government level, is closest to the people, directly articulates their needs and effects positive social consequence through good legislation. Furthermore, the Legislature aggregates the varied interests and needs of diverse peoples, spread across extensive constituencies in the country, into a composite legislative agenda for the enactment of laws that impact positively on the life, well being and welfare of all citizens.

Traditionally, legislative governance comes under three broad categories: Representation, Legislation or Law-making, and Oversight. Legislators represent their different constituencies, make laws that address critical social, political, cultural and economic issues affecting the people, and exercise an oversight responsibility over executive ministries, agencies, parastatals and extra-ministerial departments. We will also see that in, at least, two of the key functions or mandates of the Legislature – law making and oversight – a structured relationship is developed with the executive branch, which has the capacity of generating conflict.

Fundamentals of Executive Governance

While this may not appear familiar to many people because of the direct, daily impact of executive policies and decisions on the lives of the people, The executive Branch is indeed the Second, and not the First Arm of Government. Actually in the USA, which is credited with having created the first modern constitutional democracy, the Capitol Hill, which houses the Congress, and which was built with Marble and decorated with gold, looks down on the White House, which houses the presidency, built of stone and chalk. The reason for this is because the founders of the union were intent on reminding the USA President where true people power lies, in the same way that the constitution with its various amendments is replete with enough checks on the perceived monstrous powers of the Executive presidency.

The Executive branch in Nigeria, which is overseen by an elected Executive President and who is assisted by the Vice-President, Ministers and other special aides, administers the country on a day-to-day basis, and executes policies and implements programmes that are consistent with the constitution and the laws made by the legislature. The President presents an annual budget to the parliament, defends the budget, secures parliamentary approval for the appropriated sum and sets about the task of the systematic implementation of same on a set of agreed timelines and benchmarks. Because the President (the State Governor likewise at the State Assembly) must present his budget estimates before the parliament; because certain portions of the budget may become contentious and will require delicate negotiations before agreement is reached; because certain executive bills may be either rejected or amended by the parliament in favour of private member's bills; and because the legislature monitors the implementation of the budget and the overall performance of the executive branch, several layers of relationship exist between the two branches, and with this the possibility of constant or periodic conflict[6].

Contexts of Legislative-Executive Relations and their Conflict Implications

We have been able to establish in the foregoing discussion that though the constitution clearly specifies the separate, individual functions of the legislative and executive branches, there are areas where these functions overlap. This is not surprising because we have already demonstrated that the inter-dependence of the different arms and institutions of democratic governance is governed by a system of relationships. In imperative terms, while the separate, individuated constitutionally prescribed space under which each arm operates is rendered conceptually as the doctrine of the separation of powers, which achieves its meaning and significance through the operation of the principle of checks and balances, the logic of inter-dependence and inter-relationship, often times, harbours concrete conflictual elements. Some of the already indicated contexts of legislative-executive relationship thus operate in such a way as to generate periodic conflicts in the discharge of their mandates by the two arms.

In concrete terms, Nigeria's democratic experiment since 1999 has witnessed a sometimes low-level, and a sometimes heightened degree of conflict in the relationship between the Legislative and Executive branches at both the Federal and State levels (especially in incipient days). At the Federal level, the frosty relationship between the leadership of the two arms, at particular periods, led to the impeachment of two Senate Presidents, the resignation of one and a breakdown in relationship between the President of the country and two Senate Presidents. In the House of Representatives, this conflict-prone situation led indirectly to the resignation of one Speaker and a very frosty relationship between the nation's President and one Speaker of the House of Representatives. Generally, too, this situation has periodically heightened political tension, heated up the polity and nearly led to the impeachment of the nation's president himself. At the state level, the conflict of interest between the legislative and executive branch has produced varied results: the removal of several Speakers and other House Leaders, and towards the end of the Second Democratic Journey (2003-2007), the impeachment, sometimes via extra-constitutional measures, of a number of state governors by a number of State Houses of Assembly.

A close examination of these conflicts clearly demonstrates that they are related, directly or indirectly, to the following situations:

i.   The overbearing attitude of the Executive Branch in its
       relationship with the Legislative Branch;
ii.   Disrespect of the Doctrine of Separation of Powers by
       the Executive Branch in its desire to impose its will,
       tail-guide, superintendent, meddle in and control the
       decisions of the legislative branch;
iii.   Unconstitutional acts by the Executive Branch in the
       performance of its functions, its executive
       pronouncements and its policy options and thrusts;
iv.   Conflict over budgetary matters, particularly in the
       areas of budgetary estimates and sectoral allocations
       of the budget;
v.   Poor implementation of the budget and extra-
       budgetary expenditures not appropriated by the
       legislature;
vi.   Conflicts that arise in the exercise of its oversight
       functions by the Legislature;
vii.   Feeling of intimidation, blackmail and being held
       hostage expressed by the Executive Branch with
       particular reference to appropriation of fund, delay in
       the bill-making process and the screening of nominees
       by the legislative branch; and
viii. Conflictual vision with regard to social and economic
       policy in a situation in which there is a lack of
       consensus in the strategic Legislative Agenda by the
       Executive Branch, the Legislative Branch and the ruling
       party.

Strategies and Mechanisms of Resolving Conflicts between the Legislative and Executive Branches

Presented below are some of the strategies and mechanisms
that can be deployed, and some of them have indeed been
deployed in the past years, in bridging the distance between
the Legislative and Executive Branches and in resolving the
conflicts that arise in their relationship:

i.   Level-headed approach to conflictual issues by the leadership of both branches. This approach is reinforced by mutual respect and regard, attenuation of ego and the pursuit of common purposes and shared vision and values above personality clashes and antipathies.

ii.   The role of the Leadership of the various political parties, especially the ruling party, elder statesmen and opinion leaders in balancing choices and striking the middle ground of consensus and peace building between the two branches.

iii.   The office of the Special Adviser to the President on National Assembly matters, which was created for the first time during the Second Republic, is actually designed as a "go-between" between the two branches to smooth rough paths, mend fences, erase doubts and suspicious and build confidence through information-sharing and networking among key stakeholders.

iv.   A good and cordial working relationship between the chairmen and members of the various standing committees of the Legislature and the Ministers, heads of parastatals, etc. they perform oversight functions over their establishments. The key driver of this cordial relationship is the sharing of timely and adequate information.

v.   The role of the party caucuses, especially that of the ruling party, to which the leadership of the legislative and executive branch belongs. The party caucus is a sort of clearing house of ideas, a setting for the informal exchange of information, the bonding of political leaders and the exchange of confidence. An effective party caucus can contribute in resolving existing conflicts and preventing new ones from occurring.

vi.   Usually, as a last resort, the judiciary is repeatedly called upon to intervene in disputes or conflicts between the legislative and executive branch. Some of the complex issues the Judiciary have handled in recent times related to the Electoral Act, the Creation of Additional Local

Government Areas, the Powers of the State Government over Local Governments, Disbursement of Funds from the Federation accounts to the Local Governments and other constitutional issues pertaining to the separation of powers. However, judicial pronouncements never produce a win-win situation. It usually generates its own tension, resentment and mutual distrust, which find expression in newer forms of conflict.

Conclusion

Many people may not be aware of this, but the democratic process is a complex one. Its complexity stems from the system of relationship between its key elements, institutions and infrastructure. Because these are led by people with complex character traits, different backgrounds and philosophies of life and social behaviour, conflicts are bound to occur every now and then.

Democracy is also not an event; not even a series of events. Democracy is a dialogue, the bridging of distances and the sharing of common hopes and dreams. The Legislative and Executive branches must harbour these hopes and share these common values for the good of our democracy. And they can contribute to this dialogue by honouring the doctrine of the separation of powers in their mutual relations, while also recognizing the philosophy of inter-dependence of entities that binds one democratic institution to another organically, creating logic, engendering order and enabling coherence for the greatest good, for the greatest possible number in our nation.

Chapter

2

FORGING INTER-PARTY COLLABORATION AS ELECTORAL VIOLENCE REDUCTION STRATEGY

Introduction

A democratic system is defined by three inter-dependent and mutually reinforcing elements: instruments, which expresses the cogency of a legal state with all its extant rules that regulate political behaviour and action; institutions, which constitute the building blocks of democratic governance through the adherence to the determinants of the legal state; and processes, which relate to inter-connected dialogues, consensus-building and mass participation by diverse stakeholders in achieving a state of meaning and significance in the realization of the material and spiritual contents of democratic governance. In the above setting the engine of democratic governance remains the people, and with the exception of the judicial realm, and possibly certain categories of civil society, all people either belong to, or are sympathetic towards and supportive of the viewpoints, perspectives and vision of a given political party.

Political parties thus lie at the bedrock of democratic governance in a plural political tradition. Indeed, it is one of its most cogent institutions given their capacity for social mobilization, value articulation and the pursuit of power and its effects through legitimate means. The struggle for political power by political parties is the decisive element in the political process; an act that affects virtually all the people, and the character, pattern and direction of which explain, as nothing else could, the quality and content of the democratic system.

The singular importance of political parties in Nigeria's democratic transition in forging inter-party collaboration as electoral violence reduction strategy is both crucial and axiomatic. The import of this critical issue is situated within the context of Nigeria's evolving democratic tradition in that the crisis of Nigerian democracy derives significantly from the multiplicity of both intra- and inter-party violence that characterizes the contest for political power.

This violence devalues existing democratic instruments because it is opposed to the requirements of a legal state with established rules; weakens democratic institutions by establishing its own pseudo-institutional norms that negate the operation of existing traditions; and stultifies the growth of democratic process by disconnecting the people from their capacity to make informed and unfettered choices. Electoral violence in essence, not only violates the above principles of democratic governance, it also snatches away the people's popular sovereignty and will from them, while at the same time making the electoral process to be devoid of fairness, credibility and transparency. All these are apart from the physical harm inflicted on individuals, the dislocation of social and economic activities and the challenge such violent acts pose to the criminal justice system.

Apart from being fairly familiar with the operations of the INEC being, at the crucial stage in the institutionalization of the current democratic order in Nigeria, the National Secretary (as I then was) of one of the three registered political parties (PDP, APP as it then was and the AD), I was also aware that the then Chairman of the INEC and a number of his high officials knew of my modest role in forging inter-party collaboration in Nigeria some years back.

I have no doubt that shared values and reaching common grounds lie at the base of inter-party collaboration and unity through the bridging of all manners of social and political distances. The limits set by the conflict of philosophical and ideological perspectives and vision can only be attenuated through the constant nurturing of the nation's common umbilicus, which all the parties habour, and the sheer persistence in overcoming various layers of dissociations that separate one political entity from another.

In this persistent search for shared values and common grounds, a number of examples readily present themselves. With the lifting of the ban on political activities in August 1998 by the regime of Gen. Abdulsalami Abubakar, thousands of political groupings literally sprang up within the political space. The regime, given its ideological character and temperament, eventually settled for leisurely withdrawal from power under the context of an inter-elite deal-making, and the successor political elite, in turn, were able to cobble together very manageable political entities that made the transition process a qualified success. From the rumps of older political platforms such as the All Nigeria Congress (ANC), People's Democratic Movement (PDM), and Social progressive Party (SPP); from elements within factions of the Social Democratic Party (SDP) and the National Republican Convention (NRC); from within the ranks of the March – April, 1998 gave birth to G-34; and from among emergent political structures that exploited the new liberal political environment to announce their heralding and presence ultimately emerged the People's Democratic Party (PDP).

The collapse of the alliance between the Southern Leaders' Forum (SLF) and the Committee of Fused Associations (CFAs) led to the emergence of the All People's Party (APP) and Alliance for Democracy (AD) as two separate and distinct political parties. For the former, its structural embodiments accommodated the tendencies within the 13 associations that propelled it, as well as some political tendencies mentioned with regard to the PDP. For the latter, it was a simple union of the 19 left-leaning Southern political groupings led by the Afenifere and the Eastern Mandate Union (EMU), the Northern based radical, left-leaning United Democratic Congress (UDC) led by the late Amb. Tanko Yusuf and smaller political structures spearheaded by the likes of Alhaji Daiyabu.

Some notable attempts were made to create inter-party alliances and forge inter-party collaboration between late 1998 and early 1999 for two principal reasons: to create a supra-political platform that is capable of winning electoral contests, and to enable a relatively conducive environment for the intense political struggle among the elite given the fragile nature of the democratic transition. For example, the failure of the Southern-based and ideologically driven political groups to find comfortable accommodation within the PDP led to the alliance between the SLF and the CFA that generated the original APP-in-the-making. Even when that union collapsed, alliance-building measures and collaborate ventures continued to be facilitated.

The first major attempt at inter-party collaboration was that between the PDP and the AD, which was facilitated by the Awujale of Ijebuland, Oba Sikuru Adetona for nearly four weeks about October 1998, first in the home of Chief Bayo Kuku, later at the Oba's palace, and subsequently at the Gateway Hotels, all at Ijebu-Ode. The PDP team was co-chaired by Alhaji Bamanga Tukur and Mallam Adamu Ciroma and was made up of Alhaji Aminu Wali, Prof. Jerry Gana, Dr Iyorchia Ayu and Alhaji Ashrobi. I led the AD team that was made up of Chief John Odigie-Oyegun, Dr Chukwuemeka Eze, Ms Toyin Oluwagbayi, Sen. Kofo-Akerele-Bucknor, Amb. Yusuf Mamman and Dr Alex Mshelia. The collaborative agreement, which was signed by Prof. Jerry

Gana and myself never saw the light of the day because it was repudiated by the Afenifere leadership, which ultimately became the official position of the AD.

However, the failure of the PDP-AD alliance necessitated the AD's re-engagement with the APP, a unique collaboration in the political history of Nigeria that threw up the Chief Olu Falae and Alhaji Umaru Shinkafi presidential ticket. When that ticket failed to win the presidential election, the two parties decided not to press their case at the Supreme Court in recognition of the fragility and delicacy of the political transfer process and to ensure the quick withdrawal of the military from political governance with minimal stress, conflict and tension.

Today, many political parties operate under the auspices of the Conference of Nigerian Political Parties (CNPP), as their umbrella organization – another testimony to the vitality and dynamism of collaborative work among the nation's political parties. Though much work still needs to be done in generating and sustaining the necessary inter-party institutional platform and momentum that will impact positively on the electoral process, there is little doubt that such fledging effort has had a salutary impact on the character of the democratic process.

1. The Concept of Political Parties in Modern Democracies

Defining political parties is a task that seems relatively simple. Robert Huckshon (1984) provided what he called "a pragmatic definition". According to him, a political party is *"an autonomous group of citizens having the purpose of making nominations and contesting elections in the hope of securing control over government power through the capture of public offices and organization of the government".*

But embedded within any definition of a political party are several normative assumptions about what parties are and are not – and, even more frequently, what they should be. For example, if parties are to be "mediating institutions"

between the ruler and the governed, then what task should
they be performing? Do parties exist and function only
during elections? What roles should parties play in non-
election time? What should be the relationship between
parties in and out of government?

The roots of a thriving democracy are to be found in
peace, stability, law and order, as well as compliance by all
stakeholders with well-defined electoral laws and codes.
Equally vital is the quality of political opportunities for all
political parties facilitated by the existence of level playing
field to promote free, fair and credible elections and the
acceptance of results.

Apart from nominating and fielding candidates for
elections, political parties in modern times are also engines
of growth and vehicles for change and transformation of
the society. Parties are institutions of learning and
orientation that inform, shape and mould opinions on
national issues. Parties have indeed moved from the level of
informal orientation, sensitization and mass mobilization
to the level of setting up institutions where formal education
is carried out as seen in the United States, the People's
Republic of China and in the United Kingdom.

2. The Character of Political Parties in Nigeria

Since independence, political parties in Nigeria have been
structured deeply within the framework of ethnic and geo-
political configurations and tendencies. In the First Republic,
the Northern People's Congress, NPC, led by Sir Ahmadu Bello
and Abubakar Tafawa Balewa was dominated by politicians
of Northern origin; the National Convention for Nigerian
Citizens, NCNC, led by Dr Nnamdi Azikiwe had its soul in
the East, while the Action Group, AG, led by Chief Obafemi
Awolowo was controlled by the West. This trend continued
into the Second Republic as the NPN was again inclined
towards the North, the NPP towards the East, and the UPN
strongly anchored in the West. This notion of Nigeria
standing on a tripod reared its head again in 1999 when

out of the three parties then, two of them, AD and APP, went the way of the South-West and North-West respectively. The variation this time was that the ruling party PDP was more cosmopolitan and perhaps too big for any one ethnic group or geo-political zone to appropriate.

One of the defining attributes of political parties is the acquisition of character deeply anchored on ideology. Parties manifest independent identities, which become for them a passport. Apart from the parties in the First Republic, which to a significant level possessed this quality, political parties in Nigeria have largely been characterized by the apparent lack of any clear ideological inclination, and hence have suffered grossly from identity crisis. This situation arose as a fall-out of military intervention in the polity, which had the unfortunate effect of skewing the mentality and psyche of Nigerians towards material existence.

It is indeed noteworthy that the more military interventions there were, the weaker the parties became whenever democratic government returned. The parties in the Second Republic were still stronger than the parties that merely exist to contest election and win state power today. The very fact that a politician can belong to three or more political parties over a very short period of time attest significantly to this.

3. Inter-Party Collaboration

Although parties are organizations that compete against each other for political power, modern democracies require that such competitions must be healthy in order to sustain national stability. In like manner, the practice and doctrine of party opposition are integral to every democracy in order to afford the political system multiplicity of views and opinions on national issues, as well as offer alternative political platforms for governance.

The notion of party opposition is not an end in itself as it exists fundamentally to achieve the broad objectives of the country i.e. stability and development. Party opposition in a modern democracy must exist positively and constructively to engender national unity, and eschew bitterness and ranchor. It is in the light of the above that the concept of inter-party collaboration or relations has become a veritable and vital tool in the sustenance of every political system that operates in a multi-party system.

Inter-party collaboration exists on the *principle of immutability of the common purpose of governance* and the understanding and commitment of every political party towards the attainment of an irreducible minimum in the level of political stability. Democracy is promoted within a legal context underpinned by fairness, rule of law, freedom to express divergent opinions and equality of opportunities.

Consequently, all parties unite in one common goal to respect the laws of the land in all their activities, avoid all conducts and manners that are capable of destabilizing the polity, and avail their readiness for partnership with other political parties for the achievement of the common goal.

4. History of Inter-Party Collaboration in Nigeria

The history of Nigerian politics since independence has been a history of inter-party alliances and collaborations. In the First Republic, the Sir Ahmadu Bello and Abubakar Tafawa Belewa-led Northern People's Congress (NPC) went into alliance with the Dr. Nnamdi Azikwe-led National Convention for Nigerian Citizens (NCNC) to form the government. In the Second Republic, the Alhaji Shehu Shagari-led National Party of Nigeria (NPN) also went into a legislative alliance with the Nigerian Peoples Party (NPP) described by the late Maverick Politician Chuba Okadigbo as *"the accord concordial"*. In the 1999 elections, the All People's Party (APP) went into alliance with the Alliance for Democracy (AD) and presented a joint presidential candidate.

Inter-party collaboration indeed becomes not only a vital ingredient of the PDP-led government, but also an invaluable tool for harnessing national stability, unity and oneness of purpose. For the first time in the history of Nigeria, in 1999, the then President, Chief Olusegun Obasanjo took inter-party collaboration to a functional and statutory level by establishing the office of *Special Adviser to the President on Inter-Party Relations,* charged with the mandate to manage the relationship between parties in and out of government, and to evolve a sustainable framework of interaction among political parties in line with the objectives of government.

All over Africa and among emerging democracies, inter-party collaboration has become an integral factor for sustaining democracy. In Zambia, from 9 – 11 July, 2005, all political parties with representation in Parliament met together to draw up a broad programme for inter-party collaboration in order to build a more solid base for democracy. In Freetown, Sierra Leone, on 20 September, 2005, the three leading political parties came together in the session of inter-party dialogue organized by the United Nations Assistance Mission in Sierra Leone (UNAMSIL) aimed at building a non-partisan national platform for an open and free flow of communication and consultation between government and the opposition. In Ghana, all the registered political parties came together on 7 – 8 May, 2004, and established a code of conduct, to be the guiding principle for all party activities.

In all these collaborations, the critical issues of guarantee are:
1) To observe all rules and regulations relating to the conduct of elections and maintenance of public order.
2) Unhindered access to canvass for votes by all parties.
3) To publicly and without reservation, condemn all forms of violence, and pledge not to indulge in any violence or intimidation.
4) Equal access to the media by all parties.
5) A pledge to recognize the authority and responsibility of the Electoral Commission in the conduct of the election and announcement of its results.

5. Political Parties and Electoral Violence in Nigeria

Let us begin here by asking how electoral violence occurs and for what reasons. Electoral violence occurs when non-democratic means are employed by an individual or group of individuals to influence electoral results. Such means include, but are not limited to:

1. Stuffing of electoral ballot boxes,
2. Physical assault of electoral officers or members of other parties,
3. Arson and killing,
4. Kidnap of electoral officials and holding them hostage until results have been manipulated and announced,
5. Destruction of electoral materials, property etc.

The context of electoral violence has two major components:

- As a proactive measure – i.e. when supporters of a party or a candidate initiate a deliberate subversive process to manipulate the process and outcome of an election, which they otherwise are convinced would not turn out in their favour.

- As a reactive measure; - i.e. when supporters of a party or a candidate engage in violence to prevent a perceived rigging by another party, or to balance an alleged rigging.

One thing is clear from the above. The environment for electoral violence is always set and conditioned by the signals political parties send across to each other through their conducts during campaigns, or in government. It is deeply anchored on mutual fear and distrust and finds expression in the determination to win at all costs. Perhaps the most critical factor here is that at the end of the day, violence succeeds in influencing the outcome of elections. This is where the focus shifts to the electoral body. Is it that the electoral process and mechanism of INEC are too fragile that they always collapse in the face of manipulation by political parties?

A study of electoral violence in Nigeria since independence reveals one major tendency – it has always been blamed on the Electoral Commissions. There is a catch here:

- It is wrong for political parties to engage in violence to manipulate or influence results, but is it pardonable for INEC to announce a false result in an election?
- The 1983 elections that returned the Shehu Shagari-led NPN government to power were fiercely contested by other parties on allegations of mass rigging. Three months later, the government was overthrown by the military.

There was thus a high level of importance attached to the 2003 elections at the inception of this administration in 1999, bearing in mind this huge weight of history. The mandate of the inter-party office was therefore to achieve a high level collaboration among the political parties in order to break this jinx.

The office engaged in several consultations and dialogues with the parties through extensive tours, meetings, workshops, symposia, etc. For the first time in the Nigerian polity, all the existing parties found avenues to talk to one another under one setting. This created the environment and opportunity for the parties to express their opinions, demands, reservations, fears and even frustrations directly to each other and to government through the inter-party office.

Another issue of challenge to INEC and the government is to assess the present situation and find out whether the power configuration is still the same in order to find out the best strategies to achieve the same feat as in 2003.

6. Options for Achieving the Reduction of Violence in the 2007 Elections

Electoral violence has remained an option in our polity for the reason that it is rewarding, and thus attractive. As said above, if politicians or political parties know that at the end of the day, the real votes will 'count', electoral violence will become unattractive because it won't yield the desired result. INEC has repeatedly assured Nigerians that the votes in 2007 will 'count'. It is in the fulfilment of this promise that the ultimate guarantee of peaceful elections lies.

The parties have to rise above the candidates they field in elections. It is noteworthy that electoral violence is hardly a structurally planned party affair, but rather consists of acts carried out by candidates fielded by a party, in their desperation to win. The presidential system such as ours embodies very strong personality content unlike the parliamentary system, so from the point of nomination, the individual candidate designs and runs the campaign without much supervision by the party.

It has become very imperative for parties to come together and establish an agreeable code of conduct that will guide party behaviour before, during and after elections. Already smaller African countries like Zambia, Sierra Leone, Ghana, etc., have already made progress in this direction. To this effect, *it is recommended that the government, through the Inter-party office convenes an all political party summit* with the aim of getting all the political parties to agree to a code of conduct that will guide party behaviour before, during and after elections.

In like manner, an institutional effect can indeed be given to the above through the setting up of an Inter-Party Cooperation Council that will act in advisory capacity both to the parties and the government.

Conclusion

The process of institutionalizing violence-free electoral process in postcolonial Nigerian space within the grave limits set by the practice of liberal democracy has been going on for years. Several reforms of the Electoral Act have occurred in 2006, 2010 and 2011, and as of the moment the 1999 Constitution is still being reconstructed to reflect the imperatives of shared experiences and knowledge gained in the course of its implementation on this and other very cogent national agendas. The establishment of the Office of the Special Adviser on Inter-Party Affairs and the enablement of the Inter-Party Advisory Council (IPAC), are steps in the right direction. A Code of Conduct for political parties and politicians aimed at radically stemming the scourge of electoral violence has been drawn up and assented to by virtually all the political parties in the country. Yet, the reality of electoral violence, fraudulent electoral behavior and less than credible, transparent and free elections has haunted the nation between 1999 and 2011.

The real challenge has always been located in the search of balance between the self-described normative culture of the political establishment and the prevailing adverse economic and social realities that is the lot of the common folks, particularly the youth. The monopolization of political power and economic resources by a handful of the elite has shut-in the available political, economic and social spaces to the degree that mass political and economic exclusion, with the attendant absence of human infrastructure and human security, has already created its logic of fertile and volatile conflict indicators and triggers. Poverty, mass unemployment and social privations, in the absence of social safety nets, are concrete platforms for the recruitment of citizens ever willing to bear arms and unleash mayhem during elections, and in the various contexts of social intercourse and inter-group relations. Without the empowerment of the people in the direction of job creation, provision of sustainable means of livelihood and the drastic reduction of mass poverty, measures adopted at the political front aimed at reducing electoral violence will be grossly inadequate in rooting it out.

Furthermore, at present the political establishment, particularly the political parties, merely expresses the economic and corporate interests of the dominant elite classes. The competition for political power in a system substantially defined not by the contestation of ideas, philosophies and visions of governance but by an internecine, intra-class political warfare and power grab between factions of the political elite sets the scene perfectly for the deployment of extra-constitutional, and, often times, violent measures to make this perfidious end inevitable. The tragic consequence of the above scenario is the constant trumping of falsely 'deideologized' political norms by the unequal, dominant material relations that operate at the economic front.

The expectation of many is that the strengthening of the instruments and infrastructure of liberal democratic governance, the opening and expansion of economic and social spaces and opportunities, and the steady building of human security across several national frontiers will gradually re-align the political process and the entire liberal political establishment towards the direction of inclusiveness, egalitarianism and social compassion. Poverty reduction, economic self-sufficiency and the all-round improvement in the human development index will, of necessity, have a salutary impact on the health of the nation's politics and lead the charge in de-escalating electoral violence in conjunction with the measures and policies adopted at the political front.

Chapter

3

❦

DEMOCRACY, GOVERNANCE, CONFLICT RESOLUTION AND PEACE-BUILDING

Introduction

The General Ibrahim Babangida years as Head of State were defined by profound contradictory impulses, from a liberal governance philosophy propelled by leadership charisma that became consumed over time by social contradictions, which became a national imperative; from deep-seated institutional reforms at the economic and political sectors providing, as it were, the finest progressive political, social and economic blueprint in the history of Nigeria (the 1987 Political Bureau Report) that became tainted by moral, ethical and spiritual atrophies; and from an enthusiastically accepted democratic transition process that was tragically terminated with the annulment of the June 12, 1993 Presidential Election. In this grand national theatre of monumental proportions all segments of the Nigerian polity, particularly the elite classes, were deeply affected as never before in the history of Nigeria.

The Babangida years incarnated an enduring national image: the metaphor of collective guilt in the regime's effortless ease in inducting ideologically opposed entities into its inner vortex, and tarring all with its brash brush of lost innocence, never to be regained. This reality of collective and cumulative national violation is evident till today, for no matter the social spectrum on which one stands, the regime's positive and negative impacts have no known parallel in the nation's recorded history.

Yet, located firmly and centrally within this almost surreal national experience was one remarkable project, enunciated by a remarkable woman, the late Mrs Maryam Babangida, Nigeria's First Lady; a project which was absolved of the essential complications and contradictions that defined that era. Launched as a self-empowering programme for rural women, the Better Life project penetrated the core of women existence as none before it, in its all-encompassing reach and integrative intervention strategies. From capacity building training that was tailored towards skills acquisition, to the provision of micro-finance credit opportunities; from agro-based sustainable economic ventures targeted at poverty reduction to the raising of self-esteem; and from the inculcation of family values to the acquisition of leadership skills, this historic project became a progressive social therapy that ameliorated much that was glaringly wrong with the system.

The Better Life Programme was never a fanciful pastime designed to pander to the whims of a high office holder. It was rather a clear-sighted and well-focused developmental and poverty reduction programme articulated for the correction of gender imbalances in economic and social opportunities and access to sustainable livelihood. It had a deep strategic trajectory and result-oriented objectives and contributed as very little else could in raising the profile of Nigerian women and drawing attention to the diverse challenges facing them.

This venture, particularly given the additional impetus engendered by its reincarnation as a continental platform, is cogently related to the idea of Democracy, Governance, Conflict Resolution and Peace-building. The nexus between democracy and good governance and between conflict resolution and peace-building has long been established. The current national democratic project provides a secure platform for the integration of these themes into an organic agenda of national resuscitation and renovation, and for Nigerian women, in furthering those empowering thematic key to their being and existence. For, without a doubt, democracy generates those norms, values, culture, institutions and processes without which good governance, accountability, moral probity, rule of law and constitutionalism cannot triumph. And in so doing, also engenders the general and specific mechanisms and strategies of resolving disputes among peoples and entities, while building the culture of peace, tolerance and dialogue without which a nation and its people can never effectuate their possibilities.

It requires courage, vision and strategic imagination to establish a worthy connection between past causes and present desires; and insisting that the historical dialogue on the place of women in the polity and the strategies for affirming their potentials, which was initiated by the first Better Life Programme, is today sustained in a wider, much more involving context. Imperatively, without a doubt, the first Better Life Programme, which predated the Beijing Conference of 1995 by nearly a decade, was a clarion call to social, cultural, political and economic arm by a thoughtful women leadership that successfully balanced the retained interests of the male section of the polity with the need to construct an enabling environment for the realization of the yearnings and desires of women at the grassroots level.

The popularity of the programme, which the present effort is set to sustain derives mainly from its populist orientation, its touch of simplicity, the poignancy of its vision and mission, the charisma of its founder and initiator, and most importantly, the effectiveness of its implementation strategies. It is, of course, our collective expectation that past lessons well learned, depth of experiences nourished over time, tenacity of purpose and clarity of goals and objectives, which characterized the Better Life Programme of the past as a Nigerian agenda, will serve the purpose of a continental variant, given the mobilizational capacity of the new African Union charter and the New Partnership for Africa's Development (NEPAD) – two renaissance-heralding idioms in today's Africa that accord a pride of place to the contributions of women in making the African dream an objective reality.

I strongly believe that I am digressing dangerously, so let me make haste and return to the topic which is **"Democracy, Governance, Peace-building and Conflict Resolution"**. I suspect that my being then Director, Internal Conflict Prevention and Resolution in an Institute set up by the present government, and, maybe, as a politician who was fairly active during the initial transitional phase of our current democratization process may make the reader believe me an expert of inimitable standing. A disclaimer is thus necessary here. I am neither a conflict resolution expert in the professional sense of the word nor a student of democracy and government in the academic understanding of the discipline.

What I, therefore, intend to do is to share my thoughts and perceptions on this multi-thematic topic, and by so doing provide a broad road-map to women leaders who intend to pursue this discourse at a deeper, much more profound level. The four strands of this topic hang well together, not only in the context of cause and effect, but also in the inner interconnectedness and indissoluble affinities between them. In all our explications, however, we must always pose the all-important question regarding the role or place of women in them, lest our analysis hang in a state of suspended animation.

I believe that it will not be out of place if we quickly assert that democracy begins the moment dialogue is initiated; dialogue between groups and among people and entities. This dialogue does not serve its end for the sake of itself, but hopes to create an environment where processes, particularly, elections, will put in place an art of governance that derives from the image of democracy. Democracy thus generates all manners and levels of governance – executive, legislative, judicial and corporate. Yet, the construction of a democratic polity involves immeasurable sacrifices, requires the spirit of compromise and consensus, the striking of balance between personal expectations and ambition and group aspirations, and a win-win culture that includes rather than excludes. What, indeed, we are describing above is nothing short of conflict resolution, for apart from being a form of dialogue, democracy is a system of negotiation. Negotiation, we all know, is critically vital in the process of resolving conflict.

Democracy is thus as much the father of good governance, as it is the mother of conflict resolution. Of all systems of government, its essential, almost surreal paradox is that while it creates platforms for the ventilation of feelings; meaning that it inherently generates conflict, it again provides ready and efficacious mechanisms and strategies for its resolution. Finally, peace-building is a holistic agenda. It achieves its meaning and realizes its significance only in a democratic setting whereby the rules of governance are respected; and in the context in which there is the willingness to resolve conflict.

Peace-building involves the respect of democratic ethos, culture and practice. It refers to the perpetual promotion of the culture of dialogue and tolerance, and the honouring of the multi-faceted diversities that characterize our society. Peace-building also requires the services of good governance at all levels, and in every sphere, for nothing breaks a dialogue between and among people faster than contempt for the rule of law, executive excesses, legislative irresponsibility, judicial meddlesomeness and corporate lawlessness.

Though the connection that I have tried to make between the strands of my topic appears inelegant, and is somewhat tenuous, I believe that a significant portion of my thought may well have come through. Schematically represented, what I have tried to demonstrate is:

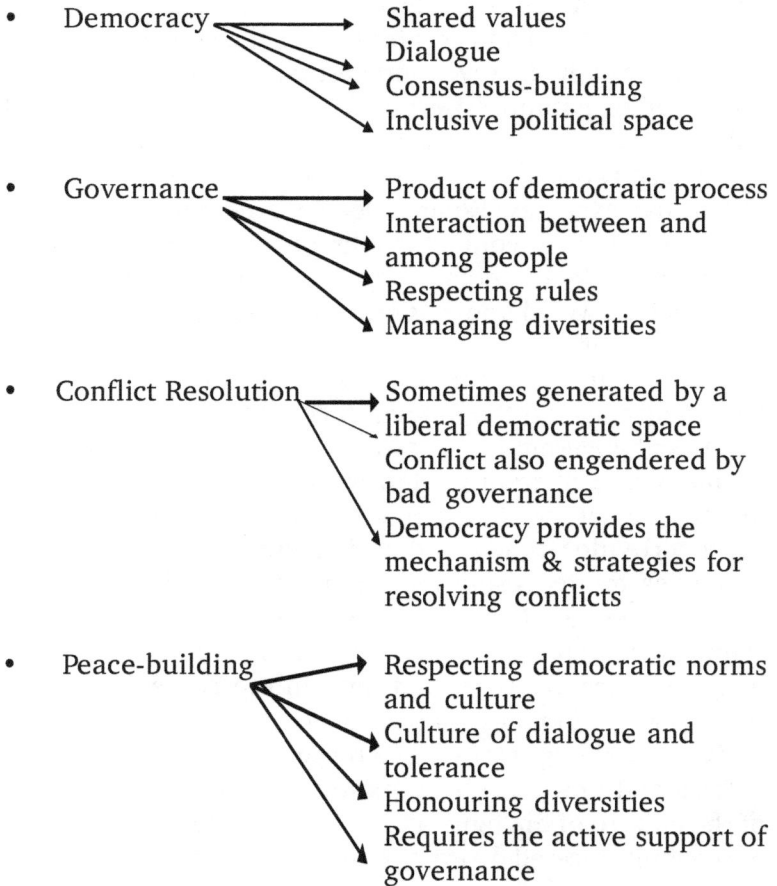

- Democracy ⟶ Shared values
  Dialogue
  Consensus-building
  Inclusive political space

- Governance ⟶ Product of democratic process
  Interaction between and among people
  Respecting rules
  Managing diversities

- Conflict Resolution ⟶ Sometimes generated by a liberal democratic space
  Conflict also engendered by bad governance
  Democracy provides the mechanism & strategies for resolving conflicts

- Peace-building ⟶ Respecting democratic norms and culture
  Culture of dialogue and tolerance
  Honouring diversities
  Requires the active support of governance

We need not search for long in order to establish the sheer interlocking connectedness of these principal thematic strands. They each rely on one another, draw strength from each other and will virtually amount to nothing without the helping hand they constantly lend themselves.

It is pertinently necessary, at this juncture, to examine

the place of women in the context of the critical issues a topic such as ours have thrown up. What for example, is the relationship between women empowerment and the democratic process? What, again, are the leadership opportunities open to women in this era of good governance, in a constitutional setting that is governed by the rule of law, equity and equal access to power? What, one may ask, has been the historical contribution of women to conflict resolution and peace-building? The next section of this chapter will examine these issues in some detail.

Democracy

For democracy to be truly a dialogue between contending interests women must give voice to their needs and anticipations, if they are to truly become integral players in the nation's democratic process. Democratic representation and participation can only be meaningful and fruitful if and only if women cease to be objects of history, and become key historical change agents. Women infuse the democratic process with humanity, vitality, and its sense of responsibility and order. While men, young and, sometimes, old, are ready to bear arms in propagating a political cause, or in canvassing for political support; and while the violence that characterizes the electoral process in usually male inspired, sponsored, led and executed, women usually settle their differences through dialogue. Without doubt, therefore, democracy as dialogue needs the services of women, their sense of decorum and their willingness to keep talking till all contending issues are disposed of. In this regard, the following suggestions will aid women participation in the democratic process, an involvement that will improve the health of other sectors of the polity as a whole:

* Education for political empowerment
* Civic training and social responsibility
* Leadership training for wholesome political participation

- Awareness of Civil Society causes and involvement in the activities of pro-democracy and human rights NGOs.

Governance

In the broadest sense of the word governance refers to the capacity of a leadership to articulate and realize a vision whose impact is directly and indirectly beneficial to those within its target range. From the home to the school; from the church to social clubs; and from corporate boardrooms to presidential power, men and women daily grapple with the issue of governance. Women are good managers, whether of their homes, their businesses, or when placed in positions of political and corporate responsibility. The quality of any given social environment is determined, substantially, by the degree to which women participate in shaping the strategic processes and events that add value to life. To the degree that women are still shut out from certain critical sectors of the national life, so long will the noted crisis of governance, which bedevils the polity, continue to endure.

There is no doubt that women have a lot of stake in determining who governs or leads them, for being society's last line of defence in the event of rupture, they fully appreciate the necessity for social order, corporate integrity and national stability. As builders and producers, in addition to their traditional role as home and environmental managers, women are well positioned to provide leadership in times of strife and change; in moments of national uncertainty; and even in period of sustainable peace and good will.

Some of the issues to be considered under governance are:

- Governance implies high quality leadership
- Governance derives from a sustainable democratic process
- Leadership training and preparation

* Maximizing strength and limiting weakness: securing positions based on talent and endowment.

Conflict Resolution and Peace-building

Women abhor war, strife and violent conflict not because of any mythical weakness, but principally because they stand to lose most in the event of social conflagration. Wars may well be fought in the battlefield but their enduring effects are to be felt at the homestead. The casualties of war are not only the maimed and the dead, but the whole of society, particularly women, who are forced to carry a burden far in excess of their capacity. Women are thus natural peace builders and conflict resolvers for it serves their purposes to ensure the reign of order and stability.

The failure of several peace-building strategies in Nigeria in the past three or so decades does not only stem from the absence of a liberal democratic space that encourages dialogue. It is also not merely the absence of good governances, as vital as this is to the idea and practice of justice, equity and fair play. This failure equally stems from the exclusion of women from the peace-building process. The idea that women are tangential in the process of resolving dispute or building peace at the community or national level – a product of a traditionalist mindset – has not only compounded the problems of conflict prevention, management and resolution but has exploded it as a myth without factual base. The very recent example of Itsekiri women who occupied an oil flow station for weeks is a case in point. In this context one can safely assert that in developing and deepening the nation's democratic process; in establishing a system of governance that is based on the delivery of social and economic dividends; and in resolving conflicts and building peace, the place of women must not only be assured but jealously safeguarded.

Some of the things to note under conflict resolution and peace-building are:

- Peace triumphs through dialogue, and democracy is dialogue
- Conflicts are natural; resolving them is also natural
- Good governance aids the building of real peace
- Women, as conflict mangers and peace builders, need peace education and specialized training and skills acquisition.
- BLP should serve as the lead national women conflict resolution and peace building agency.

It is thus clear from the foregoing analysis and the bullet points above, about the interrelationships between the different stands of our topic. I may not have made these connections and inter-links as poignantly as they should have been made. I believe that what I have tried to do is to provide us all with food for thought on the hope and expectation that a far more elegant discourse can flow out of this very imperfect analysis. And with this, I quickly move to the conclusion.

Conclusion

The Better Life Programme in the Context of the Topic

I firmly believe that, as a proactive platform, the Better Life Programme has the historic responsibility of raising the level of awareness of women on the burning issues of the day; in educating them about their place in the evolution of our democratic polity; and in instructing them about their relevance in all the different levels and dimensions of governance. Apart from providing a forum for constant, sustainable and renewable interaction and interchange of ideas and precepts, the Better Life Programme, in order to play its lead role as a women empowerment platform, must factor into its agenda the core issues that define this discourse. It must construct enduring programmes and projects that serve the interests of women as they seek a logical engagement with the democratic and other issues of our time. It ought to have a directorate or department that is devoted to the issue of democracy and governance, and another that plays up the reality of conflict resolution and peace-building.

As change agents, women need an assembly line that produces materials of all descriptions. The Better Life Programme is the women's assembly line to a great future. It can fulfil this destiny by institutionalizing a training and capacity building agenda that will be turning out, on regular and sustainable basis, women political leaders, entrepreneurs, conflict resolution experts and practitioners and all manners of peace builders. It can help in nurturing the national renewal efforts by nurturing women mangers and players in vital sectors of the economy.

Finally, by creating a liberal space in its institutional design on democracy, governance, conflict resolution and peace-building, the Better Life Programme will be factoring into the great sub-regional and continental concerns of our time, and expanding its reaches, frontiers of operation and strategic networking with other stakeholders, for within the charters of ECOWAS and the African Union, and as part of NEPAD's processes are mechanisms devoted principally, if not solely, to matters relating to democracy, good governance, conflict resolution and peace-building. If BLP taps into these platforms and becomes a core player in this field, it will not only be enhancing the capacity of its principal staff, but would be aiding the building of all round capacity of the Nigerian, nay, African women in no insignificant way.

Chapter

4

~❧~

DEMOCRATIZATION: OVERCOMING
OBSTACLES TO FREE AND FAIR ELECTIONS

Introduction

The opportunities thrown up by the current liberal political
space couldn't have been possible for free interaction, frank
exchange of views or canvassing of various positions in an
unfettered manner a few years ago. In essence, therefore,
a lot has indeed occurred in Nigeria in the past few years to
give hope to the belief that democracy can, indeed, take root
and grow, and that the current political programme would
not suffer the fate precious others did in the past. From the
death of Gen. Sani Abacha in June 1998 to the dawning of
civilian rule in May 1999; and from the first tentative,
infrastructural and institutional steps taken to the wider
dialogue engaged by Nigerian people about the bright
prospects of democracy becoming an irreversible national
political tradition, in spite of the fundamental hiccups and
obstacles strewn across its path, there are clear signs that
we are not wasting our time here, but are rather
contributing significantly in deepening and strengthening

that tradition.

There is no doubt that any meaningful discourse on democratization must engage its various institutional facets, and address issues ranged around the idea of human infrastructure and human security. Such issues as the state of the national economy; the critical agenda of poverty reduction through wealth creation; the elevation of living standard and human development index through sustainable livelihoods; and the idea and practice of good governance, constitutionalism, rule of law, due process, probity and accountability, most of which are the subject matter of discussion at this forum, are the key foundations of any genuine democratization process.

Democratization and its Two Dimensions

Democratization is a continuous and unceasing process of political and social transformation characterized by the strengthening of the structures, institutions and processes of governance in a liberal context. It has already been underscored by scholars and commentators that democratization is much more than an event, and much more than a series of loosely connected events. Democratization is an organic political and social entity in its capacity of reconciling differences, bridging distances and effecting a holistic transition from quantity to quantity and quality to quality in engendering a new social and political order.

Democratization is the conscious and deliberate design by diverse stakeholders and entities in laying the foundation of a nation of laws through the effectuation of the instruments of governance; through the erection of viable political institutions; through the establishment of a plural political state that honours dissent and divergent views; and the enablement of political succession and the acquisition of political power by free, fair, credible and transparent means that respects the sovereign will and unfettered choice of the people.

Inevitably, as the Nigerian experience reliably provides, democratization is an incremental process, and this brings us to its two principal or central dimensions. The first dimension of democratization is the transition from an undemocratic order to a nascent or fledgling democratic order or state. This has been the mantra being regularly chanted about by Nigerian politicians, media commentators and opinion molders on the need and desire to protect and safeguard Nigeria's nascent or fledgling democracy from coming to harm. This usage was very popular between 1999 and 2003. It is anticipated that as the democracy system stabilizes, the political chant will, of necessity, veer from the trajectory of protecting the nation's nascent democracy to deploying multi-layered strategies in consolidating it. Thus, the transition from nascent democracy to a consolidating democracy, with all the general and specific qualities and contents of these two political categories, explain in eloquent term the process-led, transition-based nature of democratization.

In an elite designed democratization agenda, the transition from an undemocratic order to a nascent democratic order requires the constant negotiation of interests. This situation was visibly seen with the death of Gen. Sani Abacha, the emergence of Gen. Abdulsalami Abubakar as the Nigerian Head of State and the political transition programme his regime unfolded. Even though a political stalemate occurred with Abacha's and Chief MKO Abiola's death, meaning that a negotiated democratization process could well have encompassed divergent ideological and philosophical ingredients, the regime, with its conservative and liberal civilian political backing, was able to shut out the radical, left-leaning political platforms clamouring for an alternative democratic path (a government of National Unity and a Sovereign National Conference) and successfully implemented a traditional, orthodox and conventional political succession arrangement usually associated with Nigeria's Praetorian military formation in previous negotiated political withdrawal formats.

The essential, minimal democratic demands made to and concessions granted by the negotiating regime included the following:

i.   Lifting the ban on political activities
ii.   Registration of elite political parties
iii.   Establishment of political power transfer organs (e.g. the INEC)
iv.   Enactment of a constitution; and
v.   Implementation of the transition programme that culminated with the transfer of power to a new civilian political leadership on 29 May, 1999.

It is of interest to note that the ideological, philosophical, institutional and organizational character of the participating political parties (PDP, APP as it then was and the AD) corresponded organically to these minimal requirements of democratic transition. Even though these parties owed their origins, ideological and philosophical perspectives and view-points to traditions long laid in the nation's political theatre, and drew some of their core personnel from those previous entities (NCNC, NPC, AG, NPN, UPN, NPP, GNPP, SDP, NRC, SPP, ANC, PPP, etc), the concessions made to them and which they readily accepted was the provision of a minimal liberal political space for the departure of the military from political governance and the ascension into political power of the civilian political elite. The key issues of social and political mobilization, institution building, good governance and a credible electoral system and process were deferred to a future historical date.

The second dimension of democratization is what we can conveniently classify as 'from transition to transition'; that is, the maturing stage of democratization defined by the erection of cogent and credible infrastructure and institutions of democratic governance; the operation of the rule of law and good and constitutional governance;

mobilization of civil society as a key stakeholder in democratic transformation; the implementation of broad policies aimed at social and economic renovation of society, especially the critical issue of poverty reduction through job and wealth creation (usually seen as the dividends of democracy); and most importantly, the putting in place of substantial mechanisms and institutional strategies for effecting free, fair and credible elections through a transparent electoral system and process.

Obstacles to Free and Fair Elections

It is of course a debatable issue whether by 2002 Nigerian democracy has crossed the threshold of a nascent stage to the state of consolidation. But at least on two clear, objective scores, the problematic issue of corruption, and the enduring obstacles to free and fair elections, still require a lot of work even today. Overcoming obstacles to free and fair elections is an integral part of the democratization process, meaning that as other elements that make for the sustenance of the Nigerian democratic order are refined and positioned to aid its cause, it is expected that the electoral process will also benefit from this process of refinement.

It must be noted that just as democratization, an electoral process is not a series of events culminating with the casting of votes, the counting of scores and the declaration of winners, but the merging and fusing of social and political forces to create a workable electoral climate. Elections are a crucial test of the viability and representative nature of a democratic system and, in a liberal political context, may well be the most important democratic element dealing, as they do, with popular will and sovereignty, freedom of choice in an unfettered manner, and the credibility and legitimacy of acquired political power. When obstacles overwhelm the electoral system, in which case elections are neither free nor fair, the entire democratic order loses its political and constitutional legitimacy as well as crucial moral and spiritual authority.

It will be mere wishful thinking to expect the conduct of elections to operate over and beyond the limits set by the nature of the democratic state. The nature of a polity's electoral process, including most particularly the enabling electoral law and the key arbitrator institution or political power transfer organ, is determined by the character of the democratic state. It will be too much to expect such an electoral system in such a state to achieve a heightened level of acceptable performance in a situation in which other democratic institutions and infrastructure are failing.

The reason for these limit-situations is not far-fetched. An electoral system is the sum total of the political, cultural and social values, prejudices and instincts worked into a democratic order. It is also the outward reflection or manifestation of a society's power dynamics, particularly the mechanics and strategies of power succession where a political order, and by extension, a social system is characterized by institutional corruption, dysfunctionalism and pervasive, wide-spread poverty. Furthermore, there is also the limit set by politics as an objective means of material production and a determination of upward social and economic mobility. The electoral system will, of necessity, reflect these tendencies and more. Simply put, some of the obstacles already identified with regard to the Nigerian democratic process include but are not limited to the following:

i. A weak constitutional construction with regard to the electoral system which in turn has produced a weak electoral law.

ii. A complicated elections petition judicial process which, by placing the burden of proof in electoral fraud at the same pedestal as in the criminal justice system (proof beyond all reasonable doubt), as against that placed on civil litigation (preponderance of evidence), makes it practically impossible to convict electoral offenders.

iii. A week judicial system that could easily be compromised; that lacks vigour and rigour in the application of its rules; and that sets no time limit in the disposal of election related cases.

iv. An electoral body, the INEC that is only independent in name alone, and whose key institutional, organizational, financial and personnel elements are completely aligned to and dependent on the narrow considerations of incumbent power structure to the extent that their interests are mutually inter-locked.

v. A constitutional ambiguity that led to the emergence of State Independence Electoral Commissions, a pertinently embarrassing nomenclature, given that they operate as parastatals of the various State governments and are heavily staffed with political canvassers, enforcers, informers and loyalists.

vi. The reality of politics being a means of material production and an avenue not of patriotic service but of resource agglutination which has made the competition for political offices not only a winner-takes-all affair but equally a do-or-die matter. This has made the use of violence, thuggery, intimidation, ballot snatching and stuffing, falsification of election results, etc, significant features of the Nigerian electoral process.

vii. Absence of an institutionalized inter-party collaboration platform, for the exchange of ideas and information; for the building of political synergy across party lines; for the reduction of mutual suspicion and distrust; and for the enactment of binding and enforceable code of conduct for all political parties and politicians.

viii. The endemic problem of poverty, youth unemployment and social alienation and mass disempowerment which have made many a Nigerian youth a ready material for political thuggery, violence and other criminal activities.

Overcoming Obstacles to Free and Fair Elections

I have but a brief comment to make here. The reason for this is obvious. Imbedded in the 8 obstacles identified above are located the key ingredients essential to overcoming or at least reducing obstacles to free and fair elections in the Nigerian democratic process. What I have tried to let out to the reader is to examine each obstacle closely and adopt a contrary or reverse approach in handling them. This task should be extended to the operators of the democratic system: members of the executive, legislative and judicial branches; the leadership and followership of the existing political parties; INEC officials; and members of civil society groups.

Institutionally and structurally, it is quite possible to overcome these obstacles if proper care and attention are paid to the identified limit-situations. For example, it will require enormous effort to re-construct the constitution and the electoral law that grew out of it, yet this is an imperative task that demands the co-operative labour of all stakeholders. If this is done with the independence of the INEC in mind and speedy, effective, and robust judicial intervention in election-related cases it will sufficiently address obstacles i-v. The rest of the obstacles would be addressed and overcome by utilizing the weapon of mass political enlightenment, the inculcation of positive national values, strengthening and deepening the various contexts of inter-party relations, and an aggressive social and economic programme targeted at poverty reduction, job and wealth creation and the elevation of human and living standards through policies that enhance human infrastructure and human security.

Conclusion

Elections have come to define the practice of liberal democracy in a plural, multi-party political setting. They are a key ingredient in the democratic transformation of society (democratization) and are a ready barometer in measuring the health or otherwise of any political system. As fledging as Nigeria's democratization process may be, it must begin to incorporate the needful tools and elements essential to the establishment and institutionalization, via practice, of an electoral system that is free, fair, just, equitable, credible and transparent. To do so will entail a thorough examination of the existing obstacles and a single minded application of the logic of political and social intervention in attenuating them with a perspicacity of breadth and dimension that this chapter couldn't have accomplished.

Chapter

5

THE PLACE OF THE YOUTH IN NIGERIA'S DEMOCRATIC CONSOLIDATION

Introduction

A democratic process has two distinct, though interrelated properties; the property that is rooted in the historical experience, culture, tradition and value system of a defined geo-polity and which reinforces its uniqueness and peculiarity; and the property that has universal appeal in relation to paradigms, philosophy, institutions and structures. Thus, while we can speak of the Nigerian democratic process, and by extension, the Nigerian democratic system as a unique determination of a national political ethos, we are also persuaded that that process and system are situated within the universal notion and context of liberal democracy with all its implications with regard to constitutional governance, the operation of the rule of law, respect for human rights, free, fair and credible elections and transfer of power process, among several other cogent issues.

To survive, democracy can never be an imposition from within and without. It must derive from the people's encounter with history and social being, and remains an expression of their free choice and sovereign will. Yet, in building democratic institutions on which lies the success of the democratic system, particularly at critical historical junctions, outside help may be required to subtly nudge the process along the path of self-realization. Such subtle interventions must be organically woven into the fabric of the national democratic process, and must never appear as a paternalistic, "hand-me-down", illustrationist attempt to impose alien values on a specific national temper.

This is precisely the pride of place the International Republican Institute (IRI), the National Democratic Institute (NDI), the International Foundation for Electoral Systems (IFES), the Commonwealth Secretariat and the Centre for Democracy and Development (CDD), among others, occupy in Nigeria's current democratic project. Those who are familiar with the explosion of national democratic passion between mid-1998 and mid-1999 and the single-minded commitment of Nigerians to the restoration of civil rule will acclaim the contribution of, particularly, the IRI in this direction. As the Founding National Secretary of the Alliance for Democracy (AD), my office was literally invaded by IRI staff with creative and innovative ideas about how our fledgling national democratic effort will work well.

We evolved a strong partnership based on mutual respect, and together created training, educational and voter enlightenment platforms in the form of seminars, conferences, workshops, strategy meetings, training sessions and wide distribution of voter education manuals, and several booklets dealing with political mobilization, party organization, resource management and a transparent accounting system. The IRI eventually branched into the area of conflict resolution and provided significant logistic and technical support to AD's search for internal peace and cohesion when the party was wracked by internal dissension, mutual distrust and threat of factionalization.

I took up these issues in substantial detail in my recollections of those heady days of national uncertainty, anxiety and unbelief giving way to a new season of hope and political and social becoming. Suffice it to say that it was in recognition of my modest endeavours during this period of strategic political collaboration and cooperation that made the leadership of the IRI, NED, NDI and IFES to provide a platform for me in Washington DC, USA in August, 1999 to share my experiences in the course of building Nigerian democracy to a select audience of USA executive, legislative and civil society leaders. Given IRI's track record in democratic facilitation in Nigeria and its uncommon commitment to the success of our national democratic enterprise; I am always drawn to their agenda as part of a broader process of engagements by different stakeholders in the urgent task of consolidating, strengthening and deepening Nigeria's democratic transition.

I have already stated that the IRI has been in the vanguard of building multi-layered capacity since the commencement of Nigeria's democratic transition way back in 1998. Ever since, they have impacted positively on the nation's evolving political culture, precepts and mores, be it in the area of voter education, party organization and party platforms, and conflict resolution mechanisms and strategies in a young democracy. By recognizing the central role the youth can play in the search for common grounds as Nigeria's democracy develops, IRI is always bearing a timely torch whose significance is clearly immeasurable.

What I have set out to do in this chapter is to share my thoughts, perceptions and viewpoints on a theme as challenging and stimulating as the one we have before us: "Democratic Consolidation: Youths in Democratic Action in Nigeria". The singular beauty of this theme is that it encapsulates the key ingredients germane to the successful execution of Nigeria's democratic project. These key elements, in their individuality and typicality, exemplify the

collective struggle of all democratic stakeholders in ensuring
the steady concretization of this noble ideal in our fatherland.

For a start, democracy is nothing short of a dialogue
between various social structures and institutions, and
among several stakeholders. Democracy, too, is not an event,
nor even a series of connected events, but a process-based
action plan rooted on logical ideas, and involving the exercise
of will among society's inhabitants for the realization of the
common good. Yet, this process requires steady nurture to
be consolidated, and among society's key actors, the youth
occupy a historic place in this process of social and political
renewal. To do this, they must be part of society's organic
system of deliberate action targeted at the sustenance and
irreversibility of the democratic process. You will thus affirm
with me that the combination of the key words:
"Democratic", "Consolidation", "Youth" and "Action" provides
us a broad canvas or platform on which is represented the
essential elements that will make timeless and infinite the
process the nation embarked upon since mid-1998.

Youths and Political Participation in Nigeria

The first issue that readily comes to my mind in analyzing
the role of the youth in democratic consolidation in Nigeria
pertains to the theme of participation by the Nigerian youths
in the nation's political and democratic process. Under this
context we will be examining such matters as history of
youth participation in Nigeria's political process, different
forms and levels of political participation, reasons for youth
participation, and the best practices in ensuring active and
result-oriented participation.

The fallacious notion that the youths are the leaders of
tomorrow has long been discarded by serious students of
society and the democratic process. While the youths are
the shapers of tomorrow's destiny, being history's key change
agents, they are equally fundamentally involved in today's
democratic action plans, which are central to the well-being
of the democratic state. Youths' participation in contemporary

political practices, either as leaders, canvassers, mobilizers or members of relevant civil society organizations is integral to the overall performance of the democratic transition agenda. When this participation is positive, logical and sensible, it aids the health of the democratic system. And when it is less than noble, it creates convulsions that make uncertain the democratic process.

The history of Nigeria's political process has already put a lie to the unscientific assertion that the youths are today's historical objects, while hoping for an indeterminate future time when they would become society's active subject. From the anti-colonial resistance to our present epoch the youths have been at the epicenter of democratic consolidation and concerted action. We will examine some of the highlights of this exciting historical journey:

i.   Nigeria's largest and nationally representative anti-colonial, nationalist political platform – the National Council of Nigerian Citizens (NCNC) – grew out mainly from the Nigerian Youth Movement, an association of youth activists and students who thirsted for knowledge, liberty and freedom even when some of their elders were still in slumber.

ii. The Zikist Youth Movement, a collection of radical youths who rallied under the Zikist banner, as well as the youth wings of the major pre-independence political parties (Action Group, NCNC and NPC), aided the struggle for self-rule and full independence in no mean way. They constituted the vanguard of the independence movement and canvassed for a stronger form of national sovereignty than was even achieved in 1960.

iii. At independence, and during the First Republic (1960-1966), Nigerian youths were clearly visible in institutions and structures of power as Ministers, Ambassadors, Members of Parliament and Party Leaders.

iv. During the formation of political parties in Nigeria's Second Republic (1979-1983), and in the actual business of political governance, Nigerian youths were again at the forefront of events. They brought energy, dynamism, creativity and innovation to the political process and contributed significantly to the modest achievements recorded during that turbulent era.

v. Most remarkably, Nigerian youths were to be found in the vanguard of opposition against the different military dictatorships that festered in Nigeria in the 1970s, 1980s, and 1990s. The kept the democratic flame alive, and paid great price for insisting that military rule has become an anachronism in the contemporary time. The set up barricades and manned them, protested in the streets, and died in prisons and other torture chambers built by these dictators. Here are some examples:

• The various students and civil society protests of the 1970s that climaxed with the tragic **Ali-must-go** protests of 1978.

• The various youth and civil society protests of the 1980s, the most popular of which were the SAP protests of 1986 and 1987.

• The pro-democracy and human rights platforms that fought the dictatorships of the 1990s were founded, organized and led by the youths: Campaign for Democracy (CD); Civil Liberties Organization (CLO); Committee for the Defence of Human Rights (CDHR); United Action for Democracy (UAD); and Joint Action Committee of Nigeria (JACON). Even, much more conservative pro-democracy structures like the National Democratic Coalition (NADECO) and the Eastern Mandate Union (EMU had formidable youth-based political platforms that made significant contribution to Nigeria's democratic struggle.

vi. In the current Fourth Republic, Nigerian youths are still playing recognizable roles as party activists, members of parliament and the executive branch, and in the various political-oriented civil society organizations that helped to sustain the democratic tempo and momentum. Worthy of mention here is the Transition Monitoring Group (TMG), a coalition of nearly 100 pro-democracy and human rights civil society structures.

Moreover, while it may be true that political participation relates to sustained involvement in the development of policy options, choices and actions, on the parameter that it is healthy for the youth to have a say in how their society is organized and governed, participation and the reasons for it differ from one individual to another and from one social group to another. The youth participate in politics to give themselves voice in the governance of the polity. They also participate to make a mark for themselves and achieve deeply felt inner need, expectation and desire. Participation may also occur for purely pecuniary reasons, as a means of resource accumulation and social prestige.

Yet, other categories of youth participate in the political process to provide alternative vision of democracy, achieve an alternative form of social identity, and as a means of regulating and monitoring conduct and practice. These are youths who are mostly to be found in activist watch-dog civil society groupings, and who believe that a balance must be created and achieved between the sometimes limited interests of the operators of the political system and the multivalent anticipations of diverse publics. However, whether the youth participate as active players in the partisan political environment, or as members of civil society structures, so long as their actions aid the execution of the democratic project, so long will they be contributing to the consolidation of Nigerian democracy.

There is no doubt also that participation is a form of public responsibility or civic obligation; a necessary step in the affirmation of one's individually determined but socially conditioned essence as a human person. Without full, active participation by the youth, the democratic process will be stunted in size, lifeless and lacking of vital nourishments. And because the partisan terrain is but one option in the search of social identity and the demonstration of social obligation, civil society remains a platform and an outlet for the fulfilment of collective commitment to the continued growth of the nation's democracy. At the end of the day, what is vital is that through a deliberate choice of action, one is participating in the decision making process and contributing to the consolidation of the democratic system.

Role Identification and Performance: Opportunities, Impediments and Limits

In any democratic system opportunities abound for the youth to perform personally rewarding and socially helpful roles. Equally, virtually all political systems are characterized by impediments that limit the capacity of the youth to perform the roles they desire. These impediments act as a check, a barrier or a limit-situation in the actualization of their potentials. Nigeria is no exception to this rule. While the Nigerian political system has opened up a measure of space for the youth to operate, it has also slammed the door on a number of opportunities they would desire to exploit.

For a start, many Nigerian youths feel comfortable with democratic agitation from the perspective of civil society, and there are a number of structures and platforms they can latch on to. This they have remarkably done, either as members of TMG's affiliate organizations, or as unaffiliated NGOs, CSOs and CBOs. By removing themselves from partisan bickering and narrow-mindedness, they have a better, more objective and rational insight and perspective on the events and processes of the day, and by extension will be contributing meaningfully in building and consolidating the nation's democracy.

There are yet other categories of youths who want to operate inside the political system. They emerge as the leaders of the youth sections of the various political parties where such exist. Some desire to hold elective or appointive positions and thus aspire to become local government chairmen or councillors, state assembly members or state commissioners and advisers, or members of the National Assembly. In recent times, a number of youths have been appointed Ministers, Advisers and Assistants at the federal level.

A number of barriers and impediments exist, which limit the choices open to the youth to make. Chief among this is the prejudice held by a number of older people about the capacity of youths to lead, or to have a clear voice on the great issues of the day. They thus deliberately thwart and frustrate any effort that will aid youth political empowerment. Added to this is the material implication of active political involvement, participation and role performance. In a political process that is clearly over-monetized, the material and financial challenges that the youth face are oftentimes insurmountable, thus making their activist spirit a little more than wishful thinking. The final great barrier, which is related to the one above, relates to youth unemployment and poverty. Many Nigerian youths spend all their waking moments looking for non-existent jobs or fending for their daily survival. This leaves them little or no time for full-scale involvement either in civil society movements or partisan political activities. And in a social system that fails to prepare them for self-reliant, independent economic ventures, this specific problem is greatly compounded. But as serious as these challenges and impediments are they must be mastered and overcome, if the Nigerian youth is to fulfil the role history has imposed upon them in the task of consolidating Nigeria's democracy. Some of the strategies of achieving this will be discussed in the last section of this address.

Youths and Political Violence

One of the sad commentaries on Nigeria's political process is the active involvement of youths in political violence, and all other manners of political conflicts. The youths have been the ready tool deployed by unscrupulous politicians in orchestrating an orgy of mayhem during determinate and even indeterminate political moments, particularly during electioneering campaigns and election period. The youths have been used to settle political scores, intimidate and harass political opponents, assassinate rivals, and act as thugs. This phenomenon which was a feature of the political processes of the First and Second Republics has been elevated to the level of high art in the current dispensation. Being the most active segment of the society, it is not surprising that the escalation of youth violence in the political scene has led to serious doubts about the sustainability of the democratic process. The ready availability of small arms and light weapons (SALW), and the readiness to put them to use by the youths imply that fundamental, thorough-going steps must be put in motion to curb political violence, reduce political conflicts and ensure the survival of the democratic system.

Interestingly, a number of factors account for the involvement of youths in negative political behaviour or conduct. We have already highlighted the issue of material disempowerment, poverty and joblessness. The following other tendencies are equally noted:

- A society that is driven by crass materialism, in which the attainment of material success at any cost and by all means is not a taboo or frowned upon. In the search for material means the youth lend themselves as ready agents of dastardly political acts.
- A dysfunctional social system that has thrown up a number of social abnormalities, particularly cultism amongst the youth. The various cult movements in universities, other tertiary institutions, and in the "open society" are the breeding ground of violent youths and the recruitment centre for youth-for-hire, who readily engage in political violence.
- The various ethnic, communal and sectarian conflicts across the country have led to the rise of youth militias, ethnic militias and neighbourhood vigilante structures. These groups again provide ready base for violent youths and also serve as recruitment centres of thugs

and the youth who participate in criminal political activities.

Youth Political Empowerment: Strategies and Frameworks

I will now proceed to make a few remarks on the strategies, mechanisms and frameworks of ensuring the political empowerment of youths, which will have an overall salutary effect on the democratic process. That the youths are vital stakeholders in the political system is never in doubt. This is a worldwide phenomenon, especially in the current age. To deny the youth a worthy political role to play is to create a distance between one generation and other, and once this generational gap or lacuna is created, the sustainability of the democratic process will be jeopardized. Even when they lack political experience, the freshness of youth vision, ideals and ideas; and their essential creativity, energy and innovativeness are relevant ingredients that a political system requires, and must strive to secure for itself.

Because democracy is all about dialogue, continuity and sharing of experiences, it readily implies that a vital segment of the social system – the youth – must be politically empowered to play their part in strengthening and consolidating the democratic process. If the space open to the youth is very restrictive, they will be inadequately prepared at a later time to fulfil their historic mission as change agents. Thus, the opening of political space, and youth unfettered access to political opportunities and role identification and performance are crucial steps towards empowerment.

Conclusion

I suggest, without hesitation, that the following strategies, mechanisms and frameworks be adopted to ensure that the political space accommodates the youth; that they are empowered to give voice and expression to their vision; and that they remain an integral part of the decision-making process.

- I believe that different stakeholders, including international capacity-building and democracy-support institutions, like the IRI, has an obligation in enlightening the youth about their enormous political potentials and how best to play worthy roles in the democratic process. I think that today's dialogue is a step in the right direction. Locally, the TMG can take this lead, by creating a sustainable interactive platform where youth-related issues are discussed.

- Civil society remains the main avenue or channel for the ventilation of youth viewpoints and perspectives on national issues. Enough awareness should thus be created about the capacity of civil society in aiding democratic transformation. Coalition of civil society groupings should help in setting up Youth Political Action Councils through which issues relating to role identification and performance will be constantly canvassed.

- There is also the need to strengthen the youth sections, wings or caucuses of political parties so long as these are not used to perpetrate political violence, but exist as platforms for the articulation of issues that affect the youth.

- Nigeria's poverty reduction strategy process, the National Programme on Poverty Eradication and the National Directorate of Employment, should evolve workable strategies and mechanisms of reducing poverty among the youth, increasing the rate of employment and ensuring that the youth acquire skills essential for their economic and social survival. If these steps are taken, the youth will be readily empowered to pay the necessary attention to the political issues of the day.

- Finally, the Nigerian Youth Council should be re-energized either through civil society or government initiative, or a combination of both. This council should bring together youth structures such as student bodies, Boys Scout Movement, Girls Guides, etc. This kind of platform will have the task of integrating various youth agendas with regard to civic responsibility, patriotic obligation to the fatherland, and positive social and political action with the overall objective of providing them a coherent voice on national affairs.

Chapter

6

THE NIGERIAN DEMOCRATIC PROCESS:
A NOTE

Introduction

The issues this chapter touches on are rooted in the current Nigerian democratic transition arrangement that commenced in earnest in early June 1998 with the death of Gen. Abacha and the ascension of Gen. Abdulsalami as the nation's Head of State. A combination of structural, institutional and process-based measures saw to the steady transformation of the polity from military dictatorship to civilian governance between late 1998 when the local government elections were held to late February 1999 when the presidential contest was decided.

General Abubakar's regime followed the well-established and pertinently elite-based tradition and pattern of political transfer of power by previous juntas conceptualized by some commentators as "negotiated withdraw with remarkable leisurely withdrawal properties". The essence of negotiated withdrawal was eloquently captured by General Babangida in one of his statements as Nigeria's military president when he stressed that though his regime did not know who it will hand power over to, it was fully aware and knowledgeable about those it would never hand power over to. Negotiated withdrawal strategy thus involves the careful seeking out of a malleable corps of successor civil political leaders who will reasonably sustain the legacy of the negotiating political authority; safeguard their core interests, including huge financial and material acquisitions; not seek revenge against their perceived excesses; fully protect them from harm and trial; and manage a political system in which they have a dominant influence and occupy very visible space.

Of course, the grand design of negotiated withdrawal is the use of the politics of deliberate inclusion and exclusion in attaining the objective of leadership selection and succession; that is; by including and strategically placing and enabling, via institutional measures, the civil political leaders who will take over from the negotiating regime, and by either deliberately excluding those who "will never attain power" in the regime's ideological calculation or by deploying institutional measures to thwart their political ambition, if they are not completely excluded from participating in the democratic process.

To effectuate this political strategy, the Gen. Abubakar regime enabled the following steps and processes:

1. "Lifted the ban" on political activities and thus created the space and environment for "mass" participation in the democratic process.

2. Established the major organ of political transfer of power, which it called the Independent National Electoral Commission (INEC), a misnomer in nomenclature given the fact that INEC was and remains as dependent on the incumbent political authority institutionally, administratively, financially and politically as were the FEDECO, NEC and NECON it succeeded.

3. Cobbled together a hodge-podge of previous constitutional constructions, which it passed off as a people's constitution in 1999, but which in reality was

not produced on the basis of any known mass participatory, process-led steps.

4   Published the guidelines for the registration and recognition of political parties as legal entities and subsequently registered three elite political structures; the Alliance for Democracy (AD) which leaned to the left and attained recognition as a pacification of the drivers of the June 12, 1993 election de-annulment, particularly the mainstream South-West political tendency; the All People's Party (APP), as it then was, which leaned to the right and was seen as the repository of core Northern Conservative political values; and the People's Democratic Party (PDP), an expansive, loose, ideologically un-clarified and ill-defined centrist political conglomeration that seemed to satisfy the regime's calculation on "safe landing," and which eventually attained and is still retaining national political power.

5   Published the timetable for political disengagement, which commenced with the local government elections of December 1998 and ended with the swearing in of new civilian political leaders at the state and federal levels on 29th May, 1999.

6   Finally, enabled a political environment in which both domestic and international democracy facilitators and institution builders engaged the fledgling Nigerian democratic process with diverse levels of intentions and interventions: lectures, seminars, workshops, conferences, training and strategy sessions, mass enlightenment and civic voter education campaigns, etc. The groups worth mentioning here include the Transition Monitoring Group (TMG), the International Republican Institute (IRI), the National Democratic Institute (NDI), the International Foundation for Election Systems (IFES), the Commonwealth Secretariat, the Centre for Democracy and Development (CDD), the Friedrich Ebert Foundation – Stiftung, Germany and the Konrad Adenaur Foundation.

In stressing that the current democratic process in Nigeria commenced in early June 1998 with the death of Gen. Sani Abacha I am not in any way suggesting that a democratic process is reducible to an event or even a series of loosely connected events. A democratic process is the sum total of institutional, structural, organizational and social design worked into a political system, which impact on it and is in turn impacted upon to produce a new state of reality. A democratic process is also rooted in a specific culture, value system, tradition, social psychology and inter-group, inter-ethnic and class relations even in its awareness of and response to global democratic trends. It is the complex mix of these social variables that produces the magic of democratic dialogue, democratic instruments, infrastructure and institution building and the complicated dynamics and patterns of mass responses to the issues of governance, choices and expression of sovereignty.

In essence, the Nigerian democratic process is defined by the deliberate intervention of political stakeholders in crafting a democratic society from 1960 to date. It is a convoluted, and sometimes hauntingly tragic, process that has witnessed a parliamentary democratic format (1960-1966) whose inescapable contradictions in combination with other debilitating, destabilizing and centrifugal national, social, political, economic and complex ethnic realities, saw to its abortion via a military coup d'état and the subsequent civil bloodbath it threw up (1967-1970); and the presidential democratic format of 1979-1983, which again suffered the fate of its parliamentary variant and for virtually the same mentioned reasons. Worthy of note too was the General Babangida and Gen. Abacha initiated democratic process, again, under a presidential format which collapsed with the annulment of the June 12, 1993 presidential election, and the death in office of Gen. Abacha at which stage his self-transition agenda from a military despot to a civilian leader had reached advanced stage.

While it is not my intention in this chapter to examine in detail the nature, character and essence of the Nigerian democratic process, but to indicate its major contents, it must be understood that the quality of any democratic process is measured by its organic outlook; its institutional coherence; its interconnection with mass aspirations; its bridging of distances between diverse social publics (class, ethnic, religious, cultural, linguistic, etc); its integrity in relation to the respect of popular will and sovereignty; its legal and constitutional framework and how this underscores and addresses critical societal social, political, economic and developmental challenges; and its position in relation to rule of law, good governance and respect of human and people's rights. It is by examining these categories in detail and closely connecting them to the Nigerian democratic process that would readily emerge the fidelity of that process in capturing and mastering the critical issues of the day in such a form and manner as to make future democratic and developmental interventions a settled case.

For instance, in consideration of the above viewpoints, it may be necessary to interrogate a number of issues central to the dialogue on the Nigerian democratic process. High on the list of agendas worthy of mention are the following critical issues:

1. *What is a Democratic Process?*
A democratic process is the **totality** of the **forces** and **factors** that **define, shape**, and **sustain** a democratic **system** or **order** of government. The democratic process is both **institutional** and **attitudinal**.

The institutional aspect of the democratic process pertains to the corporate **executive, legislative** and **judicial** institutions and infrastructure that energize the democratic system. The existence of a viable electoral commission and well-functioning political parties are integral aspects of this institutional design. Finally, the existence of a constitution on which is predicated the rules and regulations governing the democratic process, including but not limited to **good governance, operation of the rule of law, popular participation in policy making, national sovereignty** and **respect of fundamental human and people's rights.**

The attitudinal dimension of the democratic process in Nigeria relates to individual and collective behaviour, existence of deep-seated democratic culture and practices, the relationship between the state and civil society and the ways and means of resolving social, political and economic disputes.

2. What are the Elements that Make up a Democratic Process?

There are a number of essential elements that make up and sustain the democratic process in Nigeria. Some of the fundamental ones are:

i. **Political Parties:** Well-established, well-funded, well functioning and credible political parties is a **sine qua non** for the existence and sustenance of the democratic process, especially in a plural political tradition. Multi-party democracy is the bedrock of multiplicity of political choices in an electoral process, without which the right of people to determine who leads them is impaired. In Nigeria, even though there were initially three registered political parties and a number of other political associations seeking registration, the political party system is still very weak. In order to sustain the democratic process, political parties must be strengthened, financially/administratively/organizationally, and in terms of the generation of ideas.

ii. **Good Governance:** Good governance is a very broad field. It covers the issue of accountability and transparency, observance of the rule of law, separation of powers and the interdependence of the executive, the legislature and the judiciary. When there is good governance popular participation is upheld as a norm; there is no suppression of the people's sovereignty and the government knows that it is holding power on trust for the people.

iii. *Institutional Mechanisms:* The institutional mechanisms that help sustain the democratic process in Nigeria include an independent and credible Electoral Commission, adequacy of the existing liberal political space for capacity building (training, workshops, conferences, seminars, etc), by popular democratic institutions like the PDI, policy institutions like NIPSS, NIIA and IPCR, and the overall coordination work undertaken by the appropriate Ministry.

iv. *Relationship between the State and Civil Society:* This relationship is a vital one for the sustenance of the democratic process in Nigeria. In a democracy, the State minds its own business and occupies only the space meant for it. The same applies to Civil Societies whose members must be patriotic, truly civil, full of useful and needful civil education on obligations, responsibilities and rights of citizenship, and who must recognize and respect the authority of democratically constituted and constitutionally sanctioned governments. It is not enough for civil societies to be interested only in the rights of its members, for right without responsibility, decorous behaviour and civil conduct is mere anarchy and no democracy can survive if this were to be the case.

v. *The Democratic Process and the National Economy:* The national economy must be able to sustain the democratic process. If it is unable to do so, there is very little that political engineering and maneuver can achieve. Poverty alleviation, sustainable health and education for all, optimum employment, high standard of living, economic access for the majority of the people, low inflation rate, guaranteed food security and a healthy balance between private sector driven market economy and state control of some of the commanding heights of the economy are essential economic ingredients that can guarantee the success of the democratic process.

3.   *Sustaining the Democratic Process*
The Nigerian Democratic process can be sustained by:
- Strengthening multiparty democracy; that is, by strengthening existing and future political parties.
- Strengthening the machinery of executive, legislative and judicial governance for the promotion of the overall goal of good governance.
- Improving the all-round relationship between the state and civil society, the two principal partners in sustaining the democratic process.
- Strengthening the overall capacity of the national economy to be able to guarantee the success of the democratic process.

Conclusion
Nigeria's Fourth Democratic Republic was inaugurated on 29 May, 1999. Almost half a generation later, the democratic process still remains in a fragile state. The key instrument of democratic governance–the 1999 Constitution–has been subjected to repeated amendments and reconstructions, an exercise that is currently ongoing. Between 1999 and 2014 three different political reform, constitutional amendment and "national agenda" conferences have been operationalized as institutional undertakings aimed at re-conceiving and re-negotiating the structure, character and essence of the federal system of government.

Even with the best possible attempt at being cautiously optimistic there is a growing consensus among Nigerians that the democratization process which promised much is delivering precious little positive outcomes in the areas of the construction and legitimation of a national ideology and philosophy of governance, an empowering economic vision, policies and programmes capable of reducing poverty, ensuring sustainable, measurable and inclusive growth, promoting human infrastructure and human security agendas, and enabling a social order of national stability, peace and social security. While millions of ordinary citizens who make up over 90% of the population have been effectively shut out and comprehensively excluded from any meaningful participation in political, economic and social production of values, the democratic process has created a tiny parasitic class of very affluent citizens who have pirated and buccaneered the national patrimony with a relentless, obsessively acquisitive and degrading kleptomaniac zeal. Two logics currently define the Nigerian social space in consideration of the dominant material relations at play in its political economy of power: the culture of indolence, ineptitude, incompetence and callous indifference to the survival of the institutions of the state among the elite, and the overweening culture of monumental corruption, graft, sleaze and outright theft of the nation's wealth they have institutionalized as the defining character and essence of the state itself.

Granted that democracy is a process and not an event nor even loosely connected series of events, implying that its maturation and yield time is undefined, concrete structural and institutional signals at its moment of dawning, at its point of heralding are adequate in interpreting the decisive courses it is bound to take. The Nigerian democratic process was birthed with multiple congenital abnormalities the attenuation of which commands the people to seek a fresh procreative democratic direction. At the level of norms, as this chapter has specified, institutional measures are required to sustain its tempo and durability given the massive extent of its genetic defects, but at the level of the deconstruction of the falsely concealed ideology of the postcolonial Nigerian state whose elite delude the people that the betrayal of the norms of liberal democracy at its structural economic location is incidental and not consequential, what the people are called upon to do is a total negation of the social formation as presently constituted and the incarnation of a new egalitarian democratic path on its delegitimated and deconstructed carcass.

Chapter

7

WOMEN AND CONFLICT MANAGEMENT: THE ROLE OF LEADERSHIP, CAPACITY BUILDING AND NETWORKING

Introduction

Before venturing further with any explanation of the subject matter at hand, permit me to commend the officials of the Centre for Women Development. The women centre is an idea whose time has come. The centre has been making very important contributions in the areas of women education, gender equality, and access to political and economic opportunities, capacity building and development-based initiatives. Over the years, it has created and secured a very important national space as a reference point in women mobilization, humanitarian services and patriotic causes. An eloquent testimony to its historical relevance, clarity of definition and genuineness of purpose is ever present and increasing.

Women and children are usually victims of horrific atrocities and injustices in conflict situations. While more men are killed in war, women often experience violence, forced pregnancy, abduction and sexual abuse and slavery. Their bodies, deliberately infected with HIV/AIDS or carrying a child conceived in rape, have been used as envelopes to send messages to the perceived "enemy". The harm, silence and shame women experience in war is pervasive; their redress, almost non-existent. The situation of women in armed conflict has been systematically neglected (Elisabeth Rehn *et al,* 2002:46).

With women bearing the greatest burden of social ills during and after conflict, the chapter seeks to draw attention to a variety of strategies aimed at increasing the involvement of women in decision-making processes as well as conflict management and resolution. In particular, it looks at attempts to integrate women in the process of conflict management, and in the capacity building areas of peace building and networking.

Conflict Management: Clarification of Terms

There are several issues which come into sharp focus in considering the place of leadership, capacity building and networking with regard to the role of women as conflict managers. In examining the nature of conflict it is imperative to underscore such pertinent issues as its meaning; that is, the epistemological foundation of any discourse on the subject as well as its dynamics, patterns, trends and tempo. Properly speaking, what we are stressing here is an analysis of its complex origin and stages and dimensions of evolution. We will also be interrogating its sources and causes, which relate to both deep-rooted contradictions and complexes, and much more immediate nuances and triggers.

Of interest, too, in tackling this topic, is an examination of the place preventive and transformation techniques, mechanisms and strategies occupy in the wide spectrum of conflict management. Beginning with theoretical, methodological and analytic issues, such a discourse must, of necessity, accommodate the range of issues that pertain

to conflict anticipation, prevention, mitigation, de-escalation
and transformation through the proper understanding of
the concrete and objectively manifest nature of indicators
and triggers, the imperative of early warning signals and
the deployment of early response regimes (particularly
process-led strategies and institutional mechanisms).

Yet, another key sub-discipline that has emerged with
regard to peace and conflict studies is the issue of restorative
justice; a wholesome healing process that reconciles
offenders to victims and the community at large while not
significantly attenuating the import of retributive justice.
Central to the grand healing design of restorative justice is
the Alternative Dispute Resolution System that places
emphasis on a win-win conflict management strategy, as
well as emphasizing interest-based realities as against an
entrenched rights-based mindset. ADR as a conflict
management system accommodates such issues as
mediation, conciliation, reconciliation, negotiation and
arbitration driven by trained mediators and facilitators
whose key weapon is the constancy, regularity and
sustenance of communication channels and dialogues
between contending parties. Presently, ADR is being
systematically codified as a principal institutional set-up
through the multi-door house system; literally meaning the
existence of several doors and channels in a unified location,
but figuratively implying the existence of diverse methods
and approaches in moderating existing conflict situations.

Equally central to a deep understanding of conflict
management is the place of human security and human
infrastructure in the generation or reduction of conflict.
While traditional approaches to conflict studies readily
emphasize the importance of the maintenance of law and
order through the empowerment of the institutions and
agencies charged with this task, new paradigms broach the
same subject by emphasizing the place of development,
wealth creation, poverty reduction, sustainable livelihood,
access to health, education, electric power and water,

economic and political opportunities, justice and good governance (constitutionalism, rule of law, due process, probity, transparency and accountability) as conflict reduction strategies. Unarguably, it is by elevating human and living standards in measurable human development index (human infrastructure), that people, individually and collectively, are empowered and enabled to become active agents in building a peaceful society (human security). The maintenance of law and order, reduction of criminality and violent behaviour are coterminous with the degree with which issues evolving around human infrastructure and human security are accorded significant space and attention.

The chapter will also touch on the importance of leadership and networking in conflict management processes. Leadership is enhanced through regular and sustained capacity building and skills acquisition and enhancement in conflict analysis, preventive diplomacy and early warning and early response strategies both for government officials, key civil society leaders and operators, and the generality of women who belong to one community based organization or trust or the other. The need to enhance conflict management, improved communication, mediation and negotiation skills is imperative. But without a doubt, these knowledge and skills will have limited impact in the absence of networking, building of synergy, institutionalizing peace building coalitions and the regular sharing of ideas, information and general data.

Networking for example, dismantles artificial barriers, collapses turfs, reduces suspicion and mistrust, helps in demarcating interlocking and interconnected peace building platforms and spaces and enables instant and constant communication. These are some of the key issues the chapter will address in a broad context, with a view to opening the space for further dialogue and a more rigorous interrogation of the principal thematic content of the topic.

i.   *Conflict:* Conflict is the struggle between two opposing forces. Conflict could be over resources, ideas, values, and deep-seated needs. Conflict is normal in human relationships and serves as the motor of change. Conflict as a phenomenon provides us with great possibilities, but it is how we deal with it that can be negative or positive. The Chinese see conflict as something to be managed constructively so as to achieve positive change, development, understanding, friendship, progress, peace, communication, love, etc. Conflicts may have multiple causes. They operate at various stages of escalation or de-escalation. Interventions can be undertaken at any point in the conflict-peace spectrum and can be performed by third parties as well as by parties to the dispute.

ii. ***Conflict Prevention:*** Conflict prevention refers to actions that take place before disputes between parties become either a crisis or an active violent conflict. Conflict prevention pertains to intervention strategies before threats to use force or coercion are made or before resort to significant exercise of armed force or coercion.

iii. ***Conflict Mitigation:*** Conflict mitigation refers to actions taken to contain and reduce violence in conflicts that have already exploded. Conflict mitigation thus occurs at other points during the typical conflict life cycle, after violence has erupted.

iv. ***Conflict Resolution:*** This pertains to efforts to increase cooperation among the parties to a conflict and deepen their relationship by addressing the conditions that led to the dispute. This is also achieved by fostering positive attitudes and allaying distrust through reconciliation initiatives and building or strengthening the institutions and processes through which the parties interact. It is important to note that conflict resolution can be used to reduce the chances of violence or to consolidate the ceasation of a violent conflict in order to prevent re-escalation.

v. *Conflict Management:* Efforts to contain and if possible, reduce the amount of violence used by parties engaged in violent conflict and to engage them in communication, looking toward settling the dispute and terminating the violence.

Leadership Role

Our focus is on women as actors and not merely victims of conflict, and on women's leadership in conflict management. It is important to state the challenges of conflict management and women's leadership in the country, and also mention some of the strategies for effective conflict prevention and management by women. As earlier mentioned, because women become specific targets during wars or violent conflicts, it is therefore vital that they play a crucial role as active participants in all stages of conflict management. The following qualities are required of a good mediator in conflict situations: skills, expertise, professionalism, knowledge, moral authority, education, and social, economic and political standing. The reality is that women are part of peace processes both at the national, state and grassroots level. They engage in humanitarian assistance, child and health care as well as using traditional conflict management approaches such as the women's organizations in different parts of the country. The activities of these women are increasingly being recognized beyond the confines of their immediate environment.

The experiences of women have shown that despite their successes, particularly in grassroots mobilization and campaigning, women continue to be marginalized and ignored. The challenges they face are manifold. They seek peace for their communities. They seek peace that is rooted in social justice and freedom. And at the same time, they are struggling for gender equality against long-term structural factors which reinforce social and gender inequalities and inhibit women's leadership potential.

Capacity Building

Participation of women has generally been limited to the role of counselling other women affected by conflict, or engaging in other humanitarian-oriented activities. Although these are important, the point should be made not to replicate patriarchal division of labour in conflict management interventions by assigning women to the periphery of the political, social and cultural debate. The modern-day prevention of conflict requires the full commitment of everyone, no matter how irrelevant they might have been previously perceived. In order to achieve better results in conflict management, there is need for women in various positions/organizations to sharpen their skills by embarking on relevant training.

- Improved capacity of senior government officials and NGO leadership in applying mediation processes in conflict situations.
- Enhanced communication skills for negotiation and mediation.
- Improved skills in the management of emotions and interests of involved parties.
- Development of a better understanding of the dynamics of constructive management of inter and intra-state conflict.
- Acquisition of skills to constructively resolve issues that emerge in negotiation and peace processes.
- Train NGOs and CBOs in early warning and early response methods.

Networking

With the increase in internal conflicts, peace-building initiatives continue to be largely male-dominated and women are often absent from conflict resolution processes. At the level of civil society, however, there has been a broad-based mobilization of women for peace throughout the continent at all levels. Women have taken advantage of their enhanced roles during conflict situations and use this as leverage to campaign and advocate for peace. Women in collaboration with other allies have been actively engaged in promoting mediation, peace and dialogue often under extremely difficult circumstances. This has led to the creation of many women-led national and regional networks for peace.

- There is need to increase women's participation in key decision-making positions at national and regional levels, and include women's participation in conflict resolution at the highest levels on peace missions and negotiation. Building network among stakeholders, women leaders and followers, state and civil society, interfaith dialogue groups, domestic and international development agencies, among which are, UNICEF, National Refugees Commission (NRC), National Emergency Management Agency (NEMA), Institute for Peace and Conflict Resolution (IPCR), etc.
- There is need to build partnerships for information sharing, advocacy and proactive campaign on conflict prevention and resolution.
- There is need to launch and support a women's peace network in the country, and also build alliances with and between grassroots, national, regional and international women's groups.

However, many United Nations organizations (agencies, programmes and departments) play a key role in supporting women in different aspects of their conflict management activities by providing political and financial support, including research.

Conclusion

Managing conflicts and rebuilding societies are no longer the exclusive preserve of men. Without the participation of women in conflict management and decision-making we will never achieve the vision of a world free of the scourge of war and poverty.

Every discipline has its language or what may be termed disciplinary jargon. In this language you find concepts and terminologies that are in constant use in the field. There are concepts and terms that are common within the field of conflict management. We have been discussing some of those concepts and terminologies so as to prepare us for any conflict situation that we come across in working with groups and individuals in our chosen theme areas. This knowledge is absolutely important because of the increasing need all over the world to mainstream peace and conflict into all areas of human and societal development.

Chapter

8

❧❧❧

BUILDING THE NIGERIA OF OUR DREAM: THE ROLE OF TRADE UNIONS, CIVIL SOCIETIES AND CITIZENS

Without a doubt, the Nigerian nation-building project is at a crossroads. It is the crossroad between promise and despair; between dissonance and affirmation; between our collective historical possibility and the gradual, almost inexorable weakening of our historicist consciousness; and between the pontificating and sloganeering by our leaders on the grand themes of reconstruction, renovation and transformation and the debasing and imbecilized material circumstances of the average person. I believe that these are the hard issues placed before the present generation of Nigerians who must devise the strategies and mechanisms in providing the right solutions to the political, economic, social and cultural traumas and maladies that currently afflict the nation, most of them self-inflicted.

The Idea of a Nation

The construction of a nation begins with idea-consciousness grounded in material images and imperatives. Nations don't achieve their historic, geo-strategic and territorial expression upon the building of infrastructure and political, economic and cultural institutions. Nations begin as a conceptual design, as a paradigm of becoming located in the organized mindset of its envisioners. In 1914 the idea of a Nigerian nation as a material reality was concretized but that process took a while to occur. Under colonial imperialism the nation-building idea was rooted in formulating a strategic agenda for the efficient exploitation of natural and material resources and the suppression of indigenous sovereignties through oppressive political control. It also encompassed an economic totalizing process that bound together different levels of pre-existing social formations into the capitalist mode of production and the delegitimation of traditional philosophic, cosmogonist, spiritual, religious and artistic temper and spirit in favour of a Western-Modernist mode of thought and behaviour.

As bad as colonial imperialism was in Nigeria, and our scholars, leaders and opinion moulders never tire in educating us about its destabilizing excesses, indignities and inhumanities, it was yet a certain kind of nation-building idea rooted in the expansion of an empire with a globalist imagination. It was an idea about land and space, of immense historical possibility, and of a certain anticipated greatness in the years and decades to come. This may well be the only redeeming feature of colonialism given the tenacity with which our people—the leaders and the led— have clung to this idea in opposition to other contrary, centrifugal thoughts. We also see this in the constant celebration of the nation's indissoluble unity in diversity, our common historical heritage, our shared pains and values and the promise and possibility of our continental and global pre-eminence as the most populous black nation in the human entity.

The very topic I am dealing with drives this point home as forcefully as very few other thoughts can. Building a nation of our dream recognizes that the nation-building project begins as a dream, as an idea, a thought, a concept. But it is a dream grounded in material life, in harnessing the metaphysical substances of our being, existence and identity with the inscrutable, transcendental helping hand of The Almighty. Because of our 52 years of post-colonial inheritance, many now tend to forget that it was the dream of the nation's founding fathers and mothers that propelled us to where we are today. It was the dream of a free land and freer people, of economic prosperity and democratic stability, of a nation that is compassionate, inclusive, egalitarian, proud of its black civilization and heritage, protective of the poor and the vulnerable, and ready and able to defend its territorial integrity and collective patrimony. While the debate still rages over whether this dream has been realized or aborted over the intervening decades, it is indisputable that the post-1960 statecraft has tried to build on this notion of freedom, justice and equality, at least at the level of verbal intent.

Today, the nation grapples with several maladies including the suffocating nuances of corporate disorder and systemic dysfunction witnessed in the collapse of public infrastructure and social services, the depreciation of human infrastructure and human security (poverty, unemployment, malnutrition, infant mortality, life expectancy, political, social and economic exclusion, etc), structural disabilities and institutional inefficiency. Added to these are the daylight robbery and looting of the nation's wealth, self-cancelling insular and primordial political permutations and ideologies that split the SELF from the OTHER, and the gradual descent into a state of intolerable anomie on the heels of old and new security challenges and criminalities. These criminal activities, which are perpetrated by state and non-state actors, include human rights abuses and extrajudicial killings, extremist insurgencies, kidnappings and abductions, oil theft and sea piracy. Yet, in all these national oddities it must be noted that what is at work is not merely the weakening of the nation's history and the very notion of its reality but the steady abortion of its very idea.

Inevitably, when the idea or dream of a nation collapses, it becomes increasingly difficult if not outrightly impossible to ground it in substantial material terms in spite of persistent strivings. This, to my mind, is the tragedy of the Nigerian condition; the defeat of the very idea of the state, its sheer exhaustion under the weight of stupendous historical omissions and miscalculations and the difficulty in summoning the required agency for its re-mobilization and recuperation.

The Imperative Nation-Building Challenge

I will cast a passing glance at the issue I consider to be the critical challenge facing the nation-building process in Nigeria before devoting some space to the fundamental properties of a successful Nigerian nation-state and the role of trade unions, civil societies and citizens in realizing them. My thoughts on this matter may appear intriguing, esoteric and even far-fetched but if examined closely will be seen as centrally located in understanding when, why and how the rain began to beat the nation, at least for those who still honour deep and profound thoughts.

Let me repeat in some detail what I wrote in the introduction to this work. "The tragedy of the Nigerian state, and the persistent difficulties and setbacks in constructing a wholesome national community subsist in the distance between the 'ideas in the margin' and the indolent statecraft that powers the system. This sense of national dissonance and disconnection separates two tendencies; the intellectual strength and strategic capacity of a number of private citizens, at home and in the Diaspora, and the anti-cultural, anti-intellectual mindset of the bulk of the spiritually empty and morally sterile governing elite that rewards indolence, mediocrity, instant gratification and cargo-cult mentality. This distance must be bridged significantly for progress to be made in various national directions. Without a doubt, the worldview of the Nigerian elite must be properly defined and located so that the spirit of the contemporary Nigerian age will be unfurled. When that is achieved we will but agree with Karl Marx in the *German Ideology* that the ideas of the ruling classes are the ruling ideas in every age, and the classes which control the means of material production also control the means of ideas generation whether as social thesis, material practice or mental construct."

I continued this line of argument by further declaring that "the crisis of the Nigerian nation-state is structured as the conflict between two social forces, the first being the purveyors of true humanistic, cultural and intellectual values who insist, as marginal as their ideas and views are today, that a modern Nigerian state can only be crafted through reason and logic, intellect and superior ability, competence and cultural exposure. The second social force consist of those others, currently in the majority, who are secure in their settled indolent, anti-cultural, low-intellectual and mediocre mindset. For me, this is the greatest struggle of our time, the conflict between enlightenment, illumination and social epiphany in opposition to mindless mediocrity, obscurantism, incompetence and crass materialism that have for long seduced, ensnared and prodded an age of unreason and unbelief along the path of perdition and incoherence." My concluding remarks is that "whether we like it or not, in the long run, it will be the end result of the conflict between these opposing forces: coherence and incoherence, intellect and obscurantism, culture and anti-culture, and capacity and its lack that will determine the fate of the nation, and its authenticity as a vital social force in this century and beyond."

Tentatively, at this stage in the discourse, I can assert that in the search for a national liberationist thematics, particularly the capacity of the intellectual to unfurl the banner of human freedom with the miracle of the written and spoken word, and re-state, as I did in the introduction the profound ideas and wisdom of that brilliant Latin American intellectual and historian, Eduardo Galeano's

"In Defense of the Word" from his *Days and Nights of Love and War,* and quoted in his *Open Veins of Latin America,* Galeano avers that, "one writes out of the need to communicate with others, to denounce that which gives pain and to share that which gives happiness. One writes against one's solitude and against the solitude of others ... One writes, in reality, for the people whose luck or misfortune one identifies with–the hungry, the sleepless, the rebels, and the wretched of the earth ..."

Continuing, Galeano contends that, "our effectiveness depends on our capacity to be audacious and astute, clear and appealing. I would hope that we can create a language more fearless and beautiful than that used by conformists to greet the twilight ... Our writing should be such that 'does not propose to bury our dead, but to immortalize them, that refuses to stir the ashes but rather attempts to light the fire ... perhaps it may help to preserve for the generations to come' the true name of all things." Galeano spoke and wrote about Latin America but I am certain that his thoughts resonate here with trenchant force about our national condition not in the least dissimilar to that of that terribly violated and imbecilized continent.

Nation-Building Categories

Building the Nigeria of our dream is a function of many categories. We can begin by asking what this dream is all about; that is, its composite elements and essence. I have already alluded to some of these dream properties in the section on the idea of a nation with particular reference to the vision of the nation's founding fathers and mothers. I will now interrogate, in concrete terms, some of the nation-building categories on which must subsist the realization of the Nigeria of our dream.

i. Legitimacy of Political Authority

High on my list of these categories is the understated question of the legitimacy of Nigeria's political authority. The existence of a credible and legitimate political authority is a pre-condition for the successful execution of the Nigerian nation-building project. Political legitimacy flows from determinate forms of social relationships that are located in practical guarantees. These guarantees are essentially material in nature, subsisting, as they do, on the redemption of debts owed the people who have entered into a binding social contract with their political representatives. Political legitimacy is thus an expression of material relationship between the leaders and the led, a relationship that is characterized by the structure and nature of the social formation. A political authority loses its legitimacy when one party in the social bargain or contract fails to fulfil its obligations to the other party.

In practical terms, if a people vote for their legislative and executive representatives into office, they do so in the expectation that something concrete must return to them. If those they have elected into office fail to redeem their pledges, then they have no business staying in office. Interestingly, too, if a political system is so distorted, corrupted and unjust that the people keep on getting the same negative returns on their political investments, elections after elections, the implication is that not only are the elected representatives unfit to remain in office but that the political system itself is unfit to remain in place.

Very many readers will be wondering why I am dwelling so much on a settled issue in the Nigerian democratic process. The country has a constitution in place, elected governments at all levels and a functioning democratic system. Surely, it has met all the critical requirements of political legitimacy and, by extension, a key ingredient in the nation-building project. Let us pause for a moment and examine this issue closely. The existence of political legitimacy has very little to do with the presence of a constitution, no matter how well crafted or constructed. It also has very little in common with having elected representatives in place; representatives who indeed are produced via a constitutional (electoral) process.

Furthermore, political legitimacy is far removed from and is oftentimes contradistinctionally located in relation to democratic normativism; that is, the standard political behaviour, culture, and practices that flow from the ideological worldview of the hegemonic ruling elite that dominate the practice of liberal democracy but which is propagated not only as the worldview of the whole society but is used to conceal the gross economic and cultural inequalities in the social formation. Political legitimacy is all about political practice and political action and its direct impact on the people. If political practice, even in the context of a living constitution, results in mass poverty, massive unemployment, collapse of public infrastructure and social services, low human development index, blind stealing of public funds, lack of personal safety, rising and unchecked criminal activities, national security threats and social instability, repeatedly, and over time, the implication is that such a political system lacks any claim to legitimacy and must be done away with. The people of the then Soviet Union, Yugoslavia, Iraq under Saddam Hussein, Egypt under Hosni Mubarak and Tunisia under Ben Ali, to name but a few countries, were not blackmailed by the existence of a constitutional document and the presence of elected representatives. They did away with their political system when, as a consequence of political practice, and not in consideration of existing political instruments and institutions, they were convinced that their political system lacked legitimacy.

Let us also take a close look at the issue of constitutional governance. How legitimate is the 1999 Nigerian Constitution? A backward historical glance will reveal that sometime in 1976 a group of military dictators who were accountable to no one but themselves (the people never mandated them to seize political power on their behalf) decided to bequeath to the nation a presidential constitution in an arbitrary manner. Because the people never protested successfully over such a 'divine' document (it's only those who play God that can decide what is good for the people without their saying so) the constitution was conferred with both *de facto* and *de jure* legitimacy and was used as the fundamental document that midwifed the Second Republic of 1979-1983. With the death of Gen Sani Abacha in June 1998, the dictatorship of Gen Abdusalami Abubakar again 'divinely' dusted up the same 1979 constitutional document, tweaked it here and there and handed it to the people as the constitutional basis for the 1999 political transition.

Again, because the protests against this arbitrarily imposed document were muted, it has gone on to secure for the current democratic project its dubious legitimacy. The 1999 Constitution is an illegitimate political document in spite of the spirited attempts to amend and reconstruct it severally in the past decade and half but the people seemingly have decided to live with it, hence its dubious legitimacy. Apart from the tragic fact that no tweaking of that document can liberate more than 30% of national resources for capital projects because of its fundamentally defective premise and vision (the very basis of political practice, and the litmus test of the legitimacy of any political authority), it is a plain fact that Nigerians are living with a constitutional imposition, a document they had little say in its philosophical origin, ideological mindset and practical construction.

I will even go on to make a more audacious statement. In spite of its self-promotion, self-assuredness and even divinity, to wit, that it permits no other process of acquiring power except by precepts it has set, the reality is that, philosophically speaking, this is an empty claim and boast. The 1999 Constitution is not a people's constitution, was not constructed by them, and thus cannot make any claim that is binding on the people. The validity of such a claim rests on the people's collective desire to live with it, and thus far confer it with legitimate authority for the sake of national cohesion and social stability.

Let me quickly stress that it is not my intention to devalue the Nigerian democratic system and constitutional governance model. Far from it. My intention is that, in building the Nigeria of our dream, we cannot fail to raise the hard issues and ask the painful questions capable of seducing us out of our settled indolent mindset, our anti-intellectual readiness to accept any given political logic and our eagerness to foreclose discourse on the fundamental particulars of the national question. To make progress we must challenge complacent orthodoxies and fossilized conventionalities whether in the site of constitution making, democratic practice and the imperatives of political legitimacy.

ii. Ideology and Nation-Building

Ideology is a much used, abused and misused word and I do not intend to add to the confusion. In simple terms, ideology relates to sets of codified values and principles that have attained normative status over time. Ideology is so ingrained in the consciousness, imagination, behaviour and conduct of the individual as to appear not only an acceptable but a normal way of life. Ideology reinforces metaphysical beliefs and is a ready tool for social and political mobilization. To this extent, ideology is a powerful nation-building tool, a weapon of mass accent to the idea and dream of a nation, its historical evolution, its exceptionalism and self-re-invention ideals across several historical arcs. The Nigerian nation-building project will remain incoherent and unrealizable in the absence of a national ideology. Our unity in diversity theme is too generalized and fluid to serve as a national ideology. We must hit on a dramatic philosophic concept that carries the weight of our historical expectations and build a national ideological consensus around it. To achieve this, we many need to borrow a leaf from the ideological forces that is sustaining and driving forward several states like Cuba, Venezuela, China, and to an extent South Africa. Better still, we may examine and domesticate the American ideological notion of the 'American Dream' and 'American National and Global Exceptionalism' which has created the universal thesis of 'God's Own Country.'

But a word of caution is necessary here. Ideology is not a neutral category in the relationship between social classes and groups. Ideology has always been a potent instrument in class warfare, in the struggle between social groups with contradictory worldviews. Thus, in building a modern Nigerian state we should be mindful about which ideology we want to promote. Is it the ideology of the political elite, most of who hide under the cover of representative democracy to exploit the people, oppress them and loot their collective wealth, or the ideology of the working people, their trade unions and their civil society platforms striving to make Nigeria an egalitarian, compassionate and just society?

It is my contention that only a pro-people political, economic and social order can engender a national ideology that will serve not only the people's best interests but, more decisively, will guarantee the collective empowerment of the Nigerian state to great heights of affirmation. The reality is that ideology is related to hegemony; that is, the ability of the ruling elite to use the successful promotion of their ideology as the only legitimate reality in Nigeria, and their control over the commanding heights of the economy, the democratic process and the coercive apparatus of the state to suppress any other point of view that threatens their interests.

In building the Nigeria of our dream we should be thus mindful of the operation of false ideological premises that the people are made to contend and live with. Many values which appear normative and are taken for granted for being so are loaded with ideological nuances even when they don't appear so. This is precisely the mode of operation ideology adopts: through normative self-concealment it begins to wear the cloak of truth, as something very normal, ordinary and worthy of emulation. Very many people tend to forget that the home, schools, churches, mosques, work places, recreation grounds, the political process and the judicial institutions are sites for the formation, implantation and 'normalization' of ideology. These sites are what the French philosopher, Louis Althusser, calls the ideological state apparatuses, the benign and innocuous territories for the systematization of ideological loyalties.

However, there are limits set in the operation and efficacy of these ISA, such that the ruling elite may still call upon the services of the repressive state apparatuses (the army, police, SSS, civil defence corps, etc) to suppress the forces opposed to its core interests. One ready example that comes to mind is the behaviour and conduct of the Nigerian ruling elite during the Fuel Subsidy/Occupy Nigeria protests of January 2012. Having failed to convince the people, their trade unions and civil society groupings to buy into the fuel subsidy removal agenda through ideological persuasion the ruling elite used the RSA to unleash a reign of terror against the people. Brutal force, severe beatings, use of tear gas and water cannons, live bullets and direct invasion and occupation of the sites of protests became effective measures that were deployed to break the ranks of the people's resistance.

In building the Nigeria of our dream I will cite a few examples about the use of ideological manipulation to confuse the people, a project the Nigeria of our dream must abhor. Equality before the law is trumpeted as an axiomatic truth that the constitution guarantees when in actual fact this statement is nothing but an ideological projection in the minds of an unsuspecting people about a reality that does not accommodate them. The Nigerian judicial system, as a signification of society's political economy and social relations of production, is structured to protect the interests of the rich and powerful and to oppress the poor and the vulnerable. The same applies to the so-called anti-corruption agencies, the EFCC and the ICPC. Since 2007, the EFCC and the courts have not successfully prosecuted more than four or five of the so-called high profile cases involving powerful politicians, bankers, and major society figures. The suspects have benefitted from their strategic emplacement in the system to thwart and forestall the cause of justice.

Compare that to the goat, fowl, yam and cassava thieves convicted in their thousands over the same period or the conviction of hundreds of low-level internet fraudsters that the EFCC bandies about as a signpost of its efficiency and achievement. Consider that the maximum period the high profile detainees spend in police, prison and EFCC custody before securing their bail is usually three days to ten days, apart from the fact that most of them walk away the same day on self-cognizance. Place this alongside the tens of thousands of Nigeria's common and anonymous people who have been languishing in detention centres awaiting trial for upwards of ten years and you will begin to get the picture that equality before the law is an ideological illusion meant to confuse and deceive the people, and that the Nigerian judicial system is deliberately set up to protect and preserve the interests of the nation's ruling elite.

What obtains in the judicial system is also indicated in the economic system and the political process. Free enterprise and the private ownership of property is advertised as the common inheritance of all Nigerians, as something all should aspire to, and as a given FACT of our social system. However, this fact is nothing but ideological propaganda, a false pretence camouflaged as truth. The system is designed to impoverish, pauperize, bestialize, de-humanize, imbecilize and disempower the people who, in turn, are urged on by the operators of same system to acquire and own private property, and be active participants in the economics of production, value-addition and capital formation and accumulation. Politically, we are also told about the FACT of our freedom of political choice and the certainty and guarantee that we can aspire to any office of our choice. Yet, again, in this sermon we see ideology in operation, a category of mass deception that many people cannot even unravel.

Statistics abound that over 70% of Nigerians live below the poverty line, over 70% of the youth are unemployed with over 98% of the population just struggling to make ends meet. This system of deliberate impoverishment of the population is tailored to shut the people out of the political space through a well thought out political commercialization and monetization process. And yet, these are the people who are expected to buy party nomination forms ranging from ₦200,000 to ₦10million, mount credible campaigns, recruit and pay canvassers, enforcers and thugs, and pray that they are declared winners of the elections, failing which they have to procure the services of well-connected lawyers who know their way round the various judicial benches.

iii. Economic Prosperity

I am careful with my choice of the term economic prosperity as against the more conventional economic development or growth statistical pyrotechnics. This deliberate choice hinges on the fact that while economic development, in its vagueness, fluidity and conceptual amorphousness, may mean different things to different people economic prosperity is specific and direct in its reference. For the neo-liberal and Washington Consensus Nigerian economists and free market puritans economic development may well be measured by the 'rate of economic growth', macroeconomic and microeconomic stability, well-regulated and coherently functioning monetary and fiscal intervention policies and programmes, the marked increase in capital formation and accumulation and the heightened degree of Foreign Direct Investment in the Nigerian economy. While the above progressive statistics may be pleasing to the ears of the Nigerian ruling elite and the overlords of international financial institutions they report to and whose praises and commendations they ceaselessly seek it means nothing to the average Nigerian person who measures the performance of the nation's economy from a different perspective.

For example, the rate of economic growth conceals from the public the sectors that are growing and the wealth that is being accumulated through such growth, particularly the percentage of the population such growth impacts positively in their lives, the distribution and spread of resources, incomes, profits, utilizable capital, etc. on the basis of that growth. These statistics also suppress the relationship between economic growth and industrial degeneration and low capacity utilization, worsening unemployment, lowered living standards, deepening poverty, economic exclusion and the collapse of virtually over 80% of SMEs (small and middle scale enterprises. Stranger still is the non-acknowledgement, in the recent meeting between the Nigerian President and the World Bank Vice-President, of the gaping disconnect between the near total absence of electric power supply, youth unemployment figure of over 70%, national poverty level of over 70%, the deployment of nearly 70% of the national budget on recurrent expenditure, and possibly the outright looting of over 80% of the remaining 30% of the budget meant for capital projects, and the 'impressive' performance of the national economy and the government's transformation agenda going by the comments made by the World Bank official.

The Nigeria of our dream will not accommodate this strange logic of calculating economic growth using abstract macroeconomic and microeconomic variables that do not improve the living standards of our people. Economic prosperity will be attained through the sheer weight of policy, vision and transparent management of the national resources by a genuinely representative and accountable government. Its measureable indices will flow from the following sources. One, economic development and prosperity will remain an illusion unless and until the nation confronts and overcomes the challenges of industrialization through the building of a solid, renewable and self-reinforcing iron and steel and chemical and petro-chemical industrial infrastructure. Two, economic prosperity will also be unattainable in the absence of regular, adequate and sustainable power supply by combining traditional energy sources (hydro-electric, gas-powered, coal and nuclear) with renewable energy sources such as solar, wind, ethanol, etc.

Three, a popular democratic government must work towards the re-cast and re-shaping of the Nigerian political economy and social and economic relations of production in such a way as to leverage on adequate resources for progressive economic and social empowerment programmes while creating adequate operating space for private sector entrepreneurial initiates. Four, if the re-construction of the Nigerian Constitution is able to guarantee that over two-third of the national budget would be spent on capital projects; and if the political economic and production relations dynamics are progressive, a resource space will thus be created for massive investment in the areas of public infrastructure and social services and in the field of human infrastructure and human security (education, health services, job creation, social security safety nets.)

Five, none of these economic landmarks can be achieved at the present rate of official corruption, graft and sleaze. A viable solution to this menace is through the complete criminalization of corruption as a grave treasonable felony and the meting out of capital punishment to committers of economic and financial crimes against the Nigerian state. Having in place fast track courts solely devoted to corruption related cases that can guarantee just ten quickly executable capital punishment convictions in a year will go a long way in stemming what Chinua Achebe has already classified as Nigeria's terminal disease.

Leadership

I have constantly referred to the place of inspired, visionary and intellectually strong leadership as one of the principal drivers of the idea of a nation in virtually all the sections and sub-sections of this discourse. I will only reinforce the objective character of this premise by drawing from Prof. Chukwuma Soludo's quotation of Plato's averment on the subject in his *Thisday* article titled, "What Obasanjo and Yar'adua Told Me". Plato argued that, "just as a healthy person is governed by knowledge and reason, a just society must be under the control of society's most cultivated and informed minds, its 'lovers of wisdom'." Soludo was merely re-stressing another of Plato's thought in *The Republic* to the effect that no society can make progress, or is indeed worthy of progress, unless it is led by philosophers, or conversely, its leaders are transformed into philosophers. This is precisely the origin of the much abused term, 'philosopher-king'.

While stressing the importance of leadership in the construction of the Nigeria of our dream let us not forget that the structure, character and nature of any social formation with all its political economic and social production relations dynamic is implicated in the production and re-production of its political and other leadership categories. It is, thus, not a historical accident that the deep entrenchment and recycling of an indolent, mediocre, incompetent and anti-intellectual national political and bureaucratic leadership is indicative of the material forces at work in the Nigerian social system. The more inefficient and incompetent the managers of a system are the more their predilection towards corruption, graft and fraud. The deliberate exclusion of efficient, specially gifted and intellectually sound individuals from Nigeria's governing space is not only implicated in its crisis of underdevelopment and stalled nation-building project but must also be recognized as a consciously designed material reality.

One may even contend that the mediocritization of the entire public policy space has already become an ideological imperative, a mode of reasoning that recruits such a programme into a normative category. The 'normalization' and normativity of incompetence has now attained a degree that rejects all self-doubts about its social emplacement, reinforcing in the consciousness and imagination of the people the very idea of its irreplacibility, permanency and 'normalness'. To build the Nigeria of our dream this programme must be de-legitimated and reversed beginning with the construction of a genuinely democratic, egalitarian, and truly representative pro-people political system out of which will flow a new social and economic order with a more progressive political economy of power and social relations of production.

Trade Unions, Civil Societies, Citizens and Nation-Building

Trade unions, civil societies and citizens space in the nation-building process is quite huge and formidable. We will observe in passing the core role of the trade unions in various institutional settings (protection of the rights and welfare of workers, campaigning against unfair and unjust labour practices, championing the cause of progressive labour legislations, etc) and proceed to their more strategic mandate in building the Nigeria of our dream. An alliance of trade unions, civil society groupings and the citizens is a progressive platform for the articulation, propagation and affirmation of popular political, economic and social causes and ideals essential for the egalitarian transformation of Nigeria. The concept of the apoliticality of trade unions is an ideological weapon used by the ruling elite to shut out the unions from a decisive involvement and participation in the processes that shape the destiny of the nation. This must be resisted. The trade unions, civil society bodies and the general citizens must take a collective stand in all matters that affect the destiny of the people. The discourse over the re-formulation and re-construction of the 1999 Constitution, the allocation and utilization of national resources, and the impact of corruption on the health of the nation are but just a few of the issues that these popular structures must lend their voice and institutional weight to and play a vanguard role in their final trajectory.

The constancy, indissolubility and sustainability of a unified vanguard of these three popular platforms must be worked for, at all times. Historically, the best prospects for the mobilization of Nigerian people against injustice and oppressive rule have always occurred in the context of the ideological affinity of the workers' unions and the progressive

wing of civil society. A close consideration of the categories
of the Nigerian nation-building project will underscore the
entry space of this popular coalition in each and every single
item. Politically, this broad coalition has a role to play in the
political mobilization of the Nigerian people, in the direction of
the Constitution re-construction process, in the prudent,
efficient and judicious management of national resources, and
in holding all categories of public office holders accountable to
the social contract they freely and willingly entered with the
people. In essence, the legitimacy of the Nigerian political
authority will drive substantially from the decisive and
authoritative intervention of this broad patriotic coalition.

On the ideological front, the formation of a national
ideology is within the activist province of this patriotic force.
A national ideological consciousness that is driven by this
front has the capacity of rallying all the people around a
progressive philosophical thesis that will command the
support of the people as against the narrow ideological
formulation of the ruling elite which will but represent the
ideological world of a tiny segment of society. A formation
of a national ideology that is based on popular consensus
and which will harness the values, precepts, philosophy of
life, hopes, expectations and historical, cultural and spiritual
solidarity of all ethnic nationalities and patriotic social
groups will be the best gift this broad coalition will bequeath
the nation.

The role of this patriotic alliance in building a modern
Nigerian society is very important on the economic front.
The coalition must work towards the comprehensive
criminalization of corruption in the nation's legal statutes
both in its declaration as a high treasonable crime and the
death penalty it must be made to carry. The crackdown on
corruption will liberate billions and trillions of funds for
urgent work in the human infrastructure and human
security sector. Additionally, the labour-civil society coalition
should canvass for the restructuring of the national economy
in such a way as to attain a balance between the public and

private sectors in their various frontiers of intervention. Most, crucially, a key economic agenda of this national patriotic force is to ensure the return of the economy to the Nigerian people, to stimulate the economy into an organic productive engine and to, systematically, dismantle the macroeconomic policies that have tied the nation's destiny to the whims and caprices of imperial economic and financial institutions.

Before the labour-civil society platform can caricature the nation's current indolent, uninspired and incompetent political and bureaucratic leadership it must, first, purge its own ranks of crass opportunists, careerists and reactionary forces and elements who compromise the struggle by serving as the moles, police spies, informants and errand boys of the oppressive ruling elite. It must build a cadre of very articulate, principled, politically mature, ideologically formidable, philosophically clear and morally empowered leaders who understand their historical mission to the Nigerian people and the correct tactics and strategies essential in achieving it. From this vantage position the alliance will be well equipped in working for the enthronement of competence, efficiency and patriotic discipline in the various other national sectors.

Conclusion

In concluding this chapter, let me state in full the manifesto of a New National Beginning that I subsequently rendered in this work's Afterword. In her nation-building project, Nigeria is still in search of a theme. The sense of collective national dissociation of sensibility is explained, in part, by the absence of a coherent national ideological and philosophical platform that propels belief and faith. National values are, thus, not the systematization of the pool of values derived from the nation's ethnic, linguistic, religious and class coalitions but the interplay of semi-anarchic forces playing out on the national stage.

With defective key governance instruments, incompetent

bureaucracy, primitive public institutions and near incoherent social processes, the democratic transition, oftentimes, bears an embarrassing aura. Yet, even with the spectre of national incompleteness, the scars of a civil bloodbath, multiple military political eruptions and the pathological predilection of a bunch of its ruling elite towards social parasitism as the only marker of their covenant with the people, the nation stubbornly clings on hope.

That hopeful faith about a yearned for national elixir for the amelioration of social, political, economic and cultural maladies is both the deconstruction of the current triumph of illusion over reality, mirage over metaphysics, as well as a testament to the elemental force of humanity, in its tragic majesty and inscrutable logic. It is the idea that the people and their land will endure, because they willed it so. It is the inexplicable testimony of man's inherent indestructibility in the face of weighty challenges. It is also a manifestation of the philosophical truth that the human condition has an infinite capacity for tolerance and self-exoneration in opposition to collective immolation, the purificatory rite of which is the commitment of the many, through the social act of trans-substantiation, to cleanse a land polluted by a few, by way of collective suffering.

Without a doubt, a National Positive Force is awakening, and re-arming itself with the tools of intellect, knowledge and hard work. Either as ideas men and women, as institution builders, as guardians of the sacred human gift of freedom and liberty, or as dedicated artisans, entrepreneurs and farmers, a national ferment is in the making, mastering its course, awaiting its season, measuring its dawning ... This is the force that will guide the nation along the path of self-discovery. It is this force that will ensure the triumph of the national democratic enterprise through the liberation of the human spirit and the uncaging of human consciousness. It is this force that will make real and permanent the realization of the Nigerian possibility in a universe of quantum leaps and unceasing transformation.

Chapter

9

TRADITIONAL RULERS AND PEACE PRACTICE IN NIGERIA: EVOLVING A NEW PARADIGM OF ENGAGEMENT

Introduction

Central to the conception of this discourse is the location of peace and peace practice in a milieu that is rapidly transforming. Peace is everything. The world over, leaders who underestimate and undervalue the place of peace in human and national development, cohesiveness and survival have done so to their nation's peril.

Peace is not cheap and what is more, it is the foundation for driving any thriving society. It must also be noted that at the heart of Nigeria's underdevelopment is the absence of peace, for without peace a society striving for progress can make only apparent movements. For instance, recently, the managers of Nigerian economic infrastructure declared to the nation that the Nigerian economy is the 3rd fastest growing economy in the world. The gathering has experts in sufficient numbers and is therefore in a better position to explain why and how an economy will be growing so fast and poverty is inversely growing even more rapidly concurrently!

For peace to show a clean pair of heels in any clime, all that needs to be in place is unmitigated conflict and poor conflict resolution strategies that ultimately culminate in crises of all kinds that threaten and sometimes, destroy and consume such polities.

Many great regions and axes of the world are in turmoil at the moment and threatening the peace, security and stability of the whole of humanity itself. One is sometimes perplexed to ask, is man destined to exterminate its own species? National and international news channels are awash with the sad stories of intra- and inter-national conflicts of gargantuan proportions. The Arab spring — or Arab awakening if you prefer — may be the first of its kind in this era to jolt all right thinking people and it is not over as many more countries are waking to the reality that their peoples cannot be subjugated forever and what is more, it is no longer an Arab phenomenon. No nation is thus immune to such major social and political upheavals that, like tsunami, can sweep and knock the polity harder than many people can imagine. Yet, and most tragically, the positive political, social and economic forces that undergirded that rupture have been contaminated and overwhelmed by the explosion of deep sectarian fissures, extremist radicalization of its putative egalitarian ideology, the invasion of Arab social spaces by fundamentalist and terrorist networks, structures and cells and the strategic calculations of regional and non-regional powers who are fighting proxy wars in a number of Arab states in the name of democracy, justice and equity.

Closer home we witnessed the Occupy Nigeria protests in January 2012 where scores of people died protesting the increases in the prices of fuel as an emblematization of the exhaustion of the ideological pretence of the ruling elite and its deployment of Repressive State Apparatuses in containing mass discontent. The lesson of this conflictual situation clearly indicates that the country needs to work harder on peace by delimiting the national latitude that exacerbates confusion and conflict, and to do so, the traditional institutions and traditional rulers are key.

Traditional rulers are still highly respected in many communities, and have considerable political and economic influence. Although they have no formal role in the democratic structure, and unfortunately too, there is intense competition for royal seats amongst the infinite pool of eligible dynasts. The rulers play useful roles in brokering peace and amity between the people and the state, enhancing national identity, resolving minor and major conflicts and providing an institutional safety-valve for often inadequate state bureaucracies. In the area of security for example, the Nigeria Police have sometimes been overwhelmed and swamped by the sheer enormity of the work and new crimes, which now include terrorist threats confronting them, calling for all hands to be on deck.

Nigeria's Peace Architecture

The *tour de force* starts with delineating the nation's conflict and peace architecture. From the nature, dimensions and levels of threats that appear to be on the increase, to say that the Nigeria nation-state is crisis-ridden will be stating the obvious. There is no part of Nigeria today that is not reaping bountifully from chaos and anarchic restiveness of citizens in the area, resulting from challenges of governance and defective mechanisms in responding to the needs and aspirations of the citizenry. Thus, citizens are forced to resort to self-help, violent acts and criminal activities to make ends meet.

If we define criminality as the quality of being a criminal, it is clear enough that Nigerians are not inherently criminally minded; though that is not to say the nation does not have a fair share of criminals as found in all societies. The phenomenal growth in crimes and corruption suggests a new dimension that is pathological and demanding a different postulation in terms of etymology and sociology of crime.

Starting with the Niger Delta, it took the amnesty programme initiated by the late president Yar'Adua to contain the Niger Delta militancy caused by decades of criminal oil exploitation, and the desecration and degradation of the region and its environment. Even now, the problem is not over, as one or two militant groups do appear not to be completely reined in. Kidnapping is still rife in the South-East, South-South, South-West, and in some parts of the country as well. The communal crisis in Plateau State and some other states within the Benue Valley Belt is far from being over. Fulani herdsmen are constantly fighting around the country over grazing lands with sedentary farmers in their host communities, most notably the Tivs and the Jukuns.

And most devastating is the coming of terrorism in Nigeria. The entire country is now under the propitious violence of the Boko Haram, an Islamic sect that seeks to Islamize the entire North and ultimately the Nigerian nation-state. The sheer impossibility of their mission and the violent and elusive manner the sect pursues their agenda make their advent quite unique, potent and dangerous. Suicide bombing, which hitherto was alien to Nigeria, is now fully domesticated to the point that Nigeria has now met the standard legal requirements of a terrorist country. The capacity of the sect to bring full religious conflict in Nigeria, depending on how it is handled, is hardly in doubt and they have continued to attack churches and other places of worship.

It is particularly worrisome because the Nigerian government appears to be unsure about the right steps to take to contain the exacerbating conflicts in the land, particularly that of Boko Haram. To add to it, Christian leaders are now calling on their members to defend themselves against the rising attacks of the Boko Haram sect. Government's predilection towards negotiating with the terrorist group harbours the potential of breeding more and more of such divisive and dangerous groups across the country as a means of survival if the peace process is poorly managed. The implications of these permutations in the polity are quite ominous for a country in search of peace and development, and the traditional institution is in a position to do something.

Existing Peace-Building Mechanisms, Frameworks and Processes

The existing peace-building mechanisms, frameworks and processes are considerably defined by the logic of the maintenance of law and order. This traditional paradigm of conflict mitigation that was emplaced during the colonial period and faithfully reproduced by successive regimes, civilian and military, still dominates the official peace-building frameworks and practices. Granted, no society can flourish without law and order. But law and enforcement alone cannot succeed in a complex polity such as ours. The pursuit of law and order to the exclusion of other extenuating factors creates a top to bottom scenario that not only lacks creativity, dynamism and collective ownership of the peace-building process but also predetermines and prejudges matters pertaining to the conflict and peace spectrum from the perspective of officialdom. From the dismal results produced by this approach, it is imperative that a paradigm shift is long overdue. We need to reverse the pattern from top-bottom to bottom-up approach, where intelligence gathering, peace and amity building starts from the grassroots where the traditional rulers and traditional institutions will play a critical role.

Limits of Orthodox Peace-Building Strategies and the need for Intervention by Traditional Institutions

Nigeria is growing in complexities but surprisingly the institutions, where they exist at all, are not growing commensurately to competently rise to the growing challenges. As rightly observed by President Barak Obama of the United States in a Ghana speech a few years back, what African nations need to survive and grow are strong institutions and that is clearly in short supply in Nigeria. Those naturally existing or created by law are institutionally weakened or abandoned or subjugated to an individual's whims.

One clear example of this is the traditional institutions, which have suffered systematic annihilation since the military incursions into politics began in 1966. The argument has been that there is need to shield and isolate the traditional institutions from politics. One wonders why Nigerian leaders opt for this position while the colonial masters put the traditional rulers and traditional institutions to extensive use. My take on this matter is that the right kind of balance needs to be struck between mainstreaming traditional institutions into governance processes as integral part of the dominant material relations established by the ruling elite and insulating them from the corrosive, disruptive and contaminative realities of political involvement.

Traditional Rulers and Alternative Dispute Resolution

Alternative Dispute Resolution (ADR) (also known as External Dispute Resolution in some countries, such as Australia) includes *dispute resolution* processes and techniques that act as a means for disagreeing parties to come to an agreement short of *litigation*. ADR basically is an alternative to a formal court hearing or litigation. It is a collective term for the ways that parties can settle disputes, with (or without) the help of a third party. ADR are ways and methods of resolving disputes outside the judicial process (formal litigation – court). Because its aim is reconciliation, traditional rulers are there naturally to anchor ADR. In fact, most jobs of the traditional ruler is dispute resolution, because most of them sit in their courts daily listening to cases and taking far-reaching and binding decisions on their subjects.

Despite the historic resistance to ADR by many popular social publics and their advocates, ADR has gained widespread acceptance among both the general public and the *legal profession* in recent years. In fact, some courts now require some parties to resort to ADR of some type, usually *mediation,* before permitting the parties' cases to be tried (indeed the *European Mediation Directive* (2008) expressly contemplates so-called "compulsory" mediation; attendance at but not automatic settlement at mediation). The rising popularity of ADR can be explained by the increasing caseload of traditional courts, the perception that ADR imposes fewer costs than *litigation*, a preference for confidentiality, and the desire of some parties to have greater control over the selection of the individual or individuals who will decide their dispute.

ADR is generally classified into, at least, four types: *negotiation, mediation, collaborative law,* and *arbitration*. (In Nigeria's case, conciliation is included as well, for the special role of traditional rulers. This will be treated fully under restorative justice.) ADR can be used alongside existing legal systems such as customary and Sharia courts within common law jurisdictions such as we have in Nigeria.

ADR traditions vary somewhat by country and culture. Alternative Dispute Resolution is of two historic types. The first includes methods for resolving disputes outside of the official judicial mechanisms. Second are informal methods attached to or pendant to official judicial mechanisms. There are, in addition, free-standing and/or independent methods, such as mediation programmes and ombuds offices within organizations. The methods are similar, whether or not they are pendant, and generally use similar tool or skill sets, which are basically sub-sets of the skills of negotiation. But in our case, we are looking at the first: methods for resolving disputes outside of the official judicial mechanisms, and this pertain to traditional institutions.

The salient features of the type we envisage are as follows:

1. In negotiation, participation is voluntary and there is no third party who facilitates the resolution process or imposes a resolution
2. In *mediation*, there is a third party, a mediator, who facilitates the resolution process (and may even suggest a resolution, typically known as a "mediator's proposal"), but does not impose a resolution on the parties. In some countries (for example, the United Kingdom), ADR is synonymous with what is generally referred to as mediation in other countries.
3. In *arbitration*, participation is typically voluntary, and there is a third party who, as a private judge, imposes a resolution.

Beyond the basic types of alternative dispute resolutions there are other different forms of ADR that the traditional institution will find very useful:

- Case evaluation: a non-binding process in which parties present the facts and the issues to a traditional ruler and council who advises the parties on the strengths and weaknesses of their respective positions, and assesses how the dispute is likely to be decided if the disputants pursue their cause.
- Early neutral evaluation: a process that takes place soon after a case has been filed in court. The traditional ruler can intervene and settle the matter out of court.
- Family group conference: a meeting between members of a family and traditional ruler and council. At this meeting (or often a series of meetings) the family becomes involved in learning skills from the council for interaction and in making a plan to stop the abuse or other ill-treatment between its members.
- Neutral fact-finding: a process where traditional ruler and council as a third party, investigates and takes a position on the issue and reports or testifies even in court if need be, if that will serve justice. The neutral fact-finding process is particularly useful for resolving complex disputes.

Benefits of ADR

ADR has the following inherent benefits:
- Suitability for multi-party disputes
- Flexibility of procedure - the process is determined and controlled by the parties in the dispute
- Lower costs
- Less complexity ("less is more")
- Parties choice of neutral third party (and therefore expertise in area of dispute) to direct negotiations/ adjudication
- Likelihood of speed of settlements
- Practical solutions tailored to parties' interests and needs (not rights and wants, as they may perceive them)
- Durability of agreements
- Confidentiality
- The preservation of relationships and the preservation of reputations.

Traditional Rulers and Restorative Justice

Restorative Justice (also sometimes called "reparative justice") is an approach to justice that focuses on the needs of the victims and the offenders, as well as the involved community, instead of satisfying abstract legal principles or punishing the offender. Victims take an active role in the process, while offenders are encouraged to take responsibility for their actions, to repair the harm they've done by apologizing, returning stolen money, or community service. Restorative justice involves both victim and offender and focuses on their personal needs. In addition, it provides help for the offender in order to avoid future offences. It is based on a theory of justice that considers crime and wrongdoing to be an offence against an individual or community, rather than the state. Restorative justice that fosters dialogue between victim and offender shows the highest rates of victim satisfaction and offender accountability. From this explanation, there is no institution better placed to ensure restorative justice than the traditional institution.

According to Zehr and Mika (1998), there are three key ideas that support restorative justice. First, is the understanding that the victim and the surrounding community have both been affected by the action of the offender and, in addition, restoration is necessary. Second, the offender's obligation is to make amends with both the victim and the involved community. Third, and the most important process of restorative justice, is the concept of 'healing.'

This step has two parts: healing for the victim, as well as meeting the offender's personal needs. Both parties are equally important in this healing process to avoid recidivism and to restore a sense of safety for the victim. Various methods of restorative justice are practised; examples include victim-offender mediation, conferencing, healing circles, victim assistance, ex-offender assistance, restitution, and community service. Each method focuses on the needs of both the offender and the victim, and heals in different ways.

Restorative justice principles are characterized by four key values: first, the encounter of both parties. This step involves the offender, the victim, the community and any other party who was involved in the initial crime. Second, the amending process takes place. In this step, the offender(s) will take the steps necessary to help repair the harm caused. Third, reintegration begins. In this phase, restoration of both the victim and the offender takes place. In addition, this step also involves the community and others who were involved in the initial crime. Finally, the inclusion stage provides the open opportunity for both parties to participate in finding a resolution. The process of restorative justice is lengthy and must be committed to by both parties for effective results.

Restorative justice is very different from either the adversarial legal process or that of civil litigation. J.

Braithwaite writes, "Court-annexed ADR (alternative dispute resolution) and restorative justice could not be philosophically further apart", because the former seeks to address only legally relevant issues and to protect both parties' rights, whereas restorative justice seeks "expanding the issues beyond those that are legally relevant, especially into underlying relationships."

Similarly, citing Greif, Liebmann wrote:

> "a way of looking at restorative justice is to think of
> it as a balance among a number of different tensions:

- a balance between the therapeutic and the retributive models of justice.
- a balance between the rights of offenders and the needs of victims.
- a balance between the need to rehabilitate offenders and the duty to protect the public.
- Traditional criminal justice seeks answers to three questions: What laws have been broken? Who did it? and What do the offender(s) deserve? Restorative justice instead asks: Who has been harmed? What are their needs? Whose obligations are these"?

In criminal cases, victims can testify about the crime's impact upon their lives, receive answers to questions about the incident, and participate in holding the offender accountable. Offenders can tell their story of why the crime occurred and how it has affected their lives. They are given an opportunity to directly compensate the victim—to the degree possible. In criminal cases, this can include money, community service in general and/or specific to the offense, education to prevent recidivism, and/or expression of remorse.

In social justice cases, impoverished victims such as foster children are given the opportunity to describe their future hopes and make concrete plans to transition out of state custody in a group process with their supporters. In social justice cases, restorative justice is used for problem solving.

Restorative justice can proceed from our communities via the traditional rulers' direct involvement. In the community, the traditional ruler and council meet with all parties to assess the experience and impact of the crime. Offenders listen to victims' experiences, preferably until they are able to empathize with the experience. Then they speak to their own experience: how they decided to commit the offense. A plan is made for prevention of future occurrences, and for the offender to address the damage to the injured parties. All agree. Community members hold the offender(s) accountable for adherence to the plan.

While restorative justice typically involves an encounter between the offender and the victim, we should emphasize a programme's values over its participants. This can include programmes that only serve victims (or offenders for that matter), but that have a restorative framework. Indigenous groups are using the restorative justice process to try to create more community support for victims and offenders, particularly the young people.

Restorative Justice (RJ) Processes

Victim-Offender Mediation
Victim-offender mediation (VOM, also called victim-offender dialogue, victim-offender conferencing, victim-offender reconciliation, or restorative justice dialogue) is usually a meeting, in the presence of a traditional ruler and/or council mediator, between victim and offender. This system generally involves few participants, and often is the only option available to incarcerated offenders.

Family Group Conferencing
Family group conferencing (FGC) has a wider circle of participants than VOM, adding people connected to the primary parties, such as family, friends and professionals. FGC is often the most appropriate system for juvenile cases, due to the important role of the family in a juvenile offender's life.

Restorative Conferencing

Restorative conferencing (RC) also involves a wider circle of participants than VOM. Restorative conferences, which have also been called restorative justice conferences, family group conferences and community accountability conferences, originated as a response to juvenile crime.

An RC is a voluntary, structured meeting between offenders, victims and both parties' family and friends, in which they address consequences and restitution. RC is explicitly victim-sensitive.

The conference facilitator (Traditional Ruler/Council) arranges the meeting. In some cases, a written statement or a surrogate replaces an unwilling victim. The conference facilitator sticks to a simple script and keeps the conference focused, but intentionally does not testify. The intent is to allow subsequent conferences to succeed.

Traditional Rulers/Community Restorative Meetings

Traditional Rulers/Community Restorative Meetings can be conducted as public, face-to-face meetings. Traditional rulers may compel offenders to participate; it is expected that with time, the police may refer cases to them before charging to court, or they may engage the process outside the legal system.

Victims meet with the traditional rulers and offender. Meeting members discuss the nature and impact of the offense with the offender. The discussion continues until they agree on a deadline and specific actions for the offender to take. Subsequently, the offender documents progress in fulfilling the agreement. After the deadline passes, the traditional rulers/council submits a compliance report to the court or police, ending their involvement.

Implementing Restorative Justice

The two primary uses of traditional institutions are to manage overall behaviour and to respond to specific criminal actions and behaviour. Using restorative justice is significantly more effective over the long term. It can be difficult to implement, as such, wide changes to the culture of an institution are usually met with resistance from both the staff and the institutional population.

Predominately, restorative justice is used for the victim, specifically with a kind of mediation and/or restitution from the offender. Restorative justice is based on bringing together the victim, the offender, and the community; all have equal parts in repairing the relationships destroyed by crime. Generally, the offender is held accountable to the victim for the criminal action and accountable as well to the community. The underlying premise of restorative justice holds that all three are accountable to each other and it is the traditional ruler that is best placed to enforce it in our circumstance.

The traditional ruler must hold the offender accountable; the offender must give back in the way prescribed by the victim to make amends. Additionally, the offender must also give back to the community, as crime devalues any community. The traditional ruler and the community are accountable to the victim by assisting in enforcing any reparations agreed upon by the victim, and to the offender by helping the person avoid committing any more crime. In some cases, it may be difficult for the victim to participate in meetings directly, but the system is based on the offender being brought to face the implications of the crime.

To implement the system within a community, considerable ground work is needed. First, the traditional ruler/council has to establish what the norms are – what really goes on within the community, evaluate whether they are acceptable to the whole community, and work from there. Ideally, the community will define and establish positive norms which each person understands – the norms of Respect, Responsibility, Confrontation, Help, Trust and Support. There should be concrete definitions for these norms, and offenders in their care to these norms, establishing what may be called normative behaviour. It is likely better for an institution to decide its norms through a process.

The second aspect is to ensure that the rules support the norm and are consistent with it, to make the rules enforceable. When there are clear norms/rules for what is acceptable and unacceptable behaviour, the community members can be held accountable to live by these. This can be done in numerous ways, depending on the size of the community, the physical layout, the type, and the counselling programmes already available. Here is where the separation between a response to criminal behaviour within the community and the overall behaviour management tool becomes apparent. When used as a response to criminal behaviour, the sequence of events is: •Crime takes place; •A circle (defined below) is called, composed of the victim, offender, and people within the community; and the circle discusses what happened, and develops and executes some sort of reparation.

A circle is one of the most commonly used Restorative Justice practices, usually comprising the offender and the community and, if applicable, the victim. The offender must acknowledge the crime, the community discusses the implications, and, if applicable, the victim discusses the ramifications and the personal "cost". The circle must come to agreement on an acceptable restoration. The offender has to restore the cost, or provide a kind of compensation. The circle has regular meetings to discuss the progress, address any issues, and ultimately attempt to restore justice.

When used as an overall behaviour management tool, Restorative Justice embraces cognitive behavioural techniques (CBT) through counselling and therapy. It is based on a person taking positive actions and being able to see oneself positively. By feeling good about being positive, the person is more likely to maintain the positive behaviour.

Reducing Recidivism

Reduction of recidivism is also a goal of RJ, secondary to the restoration of offenders. Proponents argue that it can prevent reoffending and deter other potential criminals.

Critics counter that RJ does not significantly influence crime rates. Proponents aver that RJ is more effective than traditional methods, not that it leads to an absolute decrease in crime rates. The majority of the arguments on both sides, however, are theoretical, as the use of restorative practices is recent and is not widespread.

Traditional Rulers Communication and Intelligence Gathering

The role of traditional rulers in security and peace-building cannot be over emphasized. They are on ground and know their own and their own know them.   One reason for their influence may be that the people of many ethnic groups have cultural reasons to rely on their traditional rulers for information, protection, advancements and identity. For instance, by June 2010, Akwa Ibom State had 116 traditional rulers with official certificates from the state. They had received new cars on their appointment, among other perks. The chairman of the Akwa Ibom Council of Chiefs said that in return, the traditional fathers were responsible for preventing robberies and kidnappings in their domains.

This historic promise made by the traditional rulers underscores their awareness of the enormous powers to play decisive roles in curbing crimes and criminality through intelligence gathering and directly assisting the law enforcement agencies. Let this enormous potential be unleashed on the polity and the traditional institution and traditional rulers will rekindle hope and usher in a new lease of life for the nation.

Recommendations

Criminals are not spirits and live and operate among the people. Realizing this, the government of Anambra State recently made the traditional rulers the Chief Security Officers of their respective towns. The vigilante bodies are now under direct control of the traditional rulers in that state. The result of this is significant reduction in kidnapping cases, armed robberies and crimes generally. Such innovative ideas should be properly thought through and funded by the other states.

Beyond such ad-hoc measures and utilizations of the traditional institutions and traditional rulers, the nation needs to carve out a role for the traditional institution in the ongoing alteration of the 1999 Constitution.

Alternative Dispute Resolution (ADR) and Restorative Justice (RJ) mechanisms, strategies and processes should be constitutionalized and the specific role of traditional rulers in them clearly defined.

I recommend the return to pre-1966 arrangement where the regions ran bicameral legislative assemblies with House of Chiefs as an arm. Even if their work is limited at local government level, let it be constitutionally assigned. It is a constitutional matter. Before process, a nation first deals with its institutions; before the institutions, we must confront legal instruments. We expect miracle from traditional rulers yet their intervention capacities are hampered by the absence of legal instruments and institutions through which they can build peace. This issue is can be addressed in the ongoing amendment of the Constitution at the federal level, and the enactment of applicable laws/bye-laws at the state and local government levels.

Conclusion

It is crystal clear that the traditional rulers and traditional institution are grossly underutilized in Nigeria, especially in the area of peace-building, conflict resolution, security, and nation-building generally. Areas where the traditional rulers are most suited to make the difference are not limited to alternative dispute resolution, restorative justice, and intelligence gathering and so on. Though the traditional rulers in Nigeria may be said to be engaged in some of this, it is still at rudimentary level and ought to be constitutionally assigned and defined. There is also the growing need to revisit the pre-1966 Nigerian constitutional environment where traditional rulers constituted the House of Chiefs in the bicameral constitutions that operated in the regions, even if it means limiting to the LG level. The idea is to tap into the large reservoir of human resources lying almost fallow at the traditional institution. Since the traditional rulers are the ones at the grassroots, positively engaging them is the only way to bring government to the people, and that will enable the process for a transition to a more peaceful and meaningful life in Nigeria.

References

Braithwaite, J. *Restorative Justice & Responsive Regulation* 2002, Oxford University Press, at 249. ISBN 0-19-515839-3

Braithwaite, John (2004). "Restorative Justice and De-Professionalization". *The Good Society* 13 (1): 28 - 31.

Latimer, J. (2005). "The Effectiveness of Restorative Justice Practices: A Meta-Analysis". *The Prison Journal* 85 (2): 127-144.

Lynch, J. "ADR and Beyond: A Systems Approach to Conflict Management", *Negotiation Journal*, Volume 17, Number 3, July 2001, Volume, p. 213.

Suffolk University, College of Arts & Sciences, Center for Restorative Justice, "What is Restorative Justice?"

William F. S. Miles (Fall 1993). "Traditional rulers and development administration: Chieftaincy in Niger, Nigeria, and Vanuatu". *Studies in Comparative International Deelopment (SCID)*, Volume 28, Number 3, 31–50. http://www.springerlink.com/content/c0h122841575j654/. Retrieved 3 September 2010.

Zehr, H. & Mika, A. (2008). *Changing Lenses: A New Focus for Crime and Justice*, Scottdale, PA: Herald Press.

Chapter

10

IDENTIFYING, MANAGING AND MITIGATING CONFLICTS BETWEEN LOCAL GOVERNMENTS' LEGISLATIVE AND EXECUTIVE BRANCHES IN NIGERIA

Introduction

A close look at the 1999 Constitution clearly shows that the local government system suffers from an arrested structural and institutional development, dwelling in a world of suspended political, constitutional and administrative animation between the excessive political and financial clout of the federal centre and the increasingly authoritarian administrative syndrome that defines the governance of very many states. It would be wrong to assume that the local government system is a constitutional after thought. Those who hold tenaciously to this view fail to see that the very presence of local governments in the Constitution is a studied concession to the nation's regionalist-federalist colonial and immediate postcolonial past by a commandist junta hegemony that bestrode the political space for so long, and constructed the 1999 Constitution as their legacy to Nigeria's political development as they saw it.

Many of Nigeria's political elite believe that empowering the local government system politically, administratively and financially is conterminous with disempowering the centre and the states as federating units, forgetting that the structural and institutional tenets of true federalism lie in making the centre relatively unattractive. The whole issue of fiscal federalism, resource generation, mobilization, allocation and distribution is central to this debate for the very fact that resources are drained from the local communities which make up the local government system, centralized in the federation account, and shared and utilized in a trickle down pattern to the very communities that created or generated them in the first place. Were the nation's fiscal policy to be reversed, the whole issue of Accountants-General of the states gathering every month in Abuja to share money; the whole issue of what to do with "excess crude oil revenue"; and the inexplicable awarding of hundreds of millions of retirement, housing and pension benefits to state governors and their deputies in the specific context in which their internally generated revenue for the whole of their tenure is less than 5% of the awarded money, would be a thing of the past. This is because the local communities would be retaining substantial part of the revenue they generate, while passing on the rest to the State and Federal governments enough to service their constitutionally prescribed obligations and responsibilities.

I fully appreciate that the above comments are still academic because the Constitution still remains unamended and one doubts the political will and federalist conscience of its reframers to do the right thing. However, it is important for us to appreciate the damage the current system has inflicted on the whole issue of wealth creation, poverty reduction and resource utilization. Nigerians are tragically disconnected from their wealth, seeing in the monthly sharing of national revenue by state governors and the end to which they put such funds, as an act of benevolence. Because this connection is lacking, compounded as the problem is by the sourcing of a mono-cultural revenue from a tiny parchment of the nation, the people indeed lack the moral authority to hold their leaders accountable for their conducts and the scandalous buccaneering of the nation's wealth at the hands of a few individuals.

The local government system is the most important tier of governance, yet very many local governments are veritable wasteland, suffocated by political, economic, social and developmental neglect and presided over by absentee Chairmen who appear once every month to pay workers salaries and maintain a few essential services. However, being closest to the people, the impact of local government administration should be immediate and instantaneous, but with the national developmental paradigm becoming increasingly paternalistic, Nigerians who dwell in the rural areas are nothing short of objects of history and social experience.

This current situation is dissimilar to what obtained in the early 1970s in the then East-Central State with the introduction of the Community Council System that placed the people and their elected representatives at the centre of development and mass empowerment initiatives and agendas. The Community Council System evolved a pro-people, people-led and people-determined developmental choice which was vigorously debated at the clan or kindred level, systematized and codified at the community level, and subsequently transmitted to the local government headquarters as the people's ultimate charter of demand. I can speak authoritatively on this, because as a young boy growing up in a rural community, I observed this system and process at close quarters, my father being a two-time elected Chairman of Mgbowo Community Council. The spirit of dialogue, robust discussion, argument and consensus-building that preceded the adoption of resolutions has no comparison today. It has readily been attested that the golden age in community development in my rural environment, as in other rural communities in Igboland, was indeed the age of the Community Council System.

In addressing the issue of managing and mitigating the conflicts in Nigeria's underdeveloped local government system, I urge Nigerians to spare a thought on the Community Council System in their search for a creative approach in addressing the crisis of rural development in Nigeria, and to the Federal Lawmakers in searching out existing documents on the subject which may inform the re-construction of the 1999 Constitution as it pertains to the local government tier.

The local government council is the third tier of the federal structure in Nigeria. A local government or district or divisional council is a mini-government serving a particular unit of administrative division in a country. In creating local government councils, a country is broken into smaller units for effective administration and for access of the local people to governance, who themselves become deeply involved in the day-day affairs of their political environment. People are elected to function and undertake responsibilities and exercise powers on behalf of their people. A local government exists for the people and its main objectives are the overall development of the local community, provide channel of communication between local communities and governments at the state and federal levels, facilitate democratic self-government close to the grassroots level of the society, and encourage economic, social and cultural initiatives.

However, the local government councils instead of heading towards development find themselves in conflict over scarce resources meant for development. This chapter will, therefore, look at the roles of the Executive and Legislative organs of the local government, the conflict situations that arise in their inter-relationship and the mechanisms and strategies of resolving them.

Role of Local Government Legislative Councils

The duties of the Councillors at the local government level include the following:

*   Enact budget
*   Define powers, functions and duties of local government council officers and employees
*   Enter into contracts
*   Regulate the acquisition, sale, ownership and the disposal of local government property
*   Provide governmental recreational, educational, cultural and social services
*   Impose taxes not prohibited by the state
*   Cause the local government to run and operate utilities
*   License for the purpose of revenue and regulate any type of business
*   Enact rules governing its procedures, including public meetings and hearings.

Role of Local Government Executive Branch

The executive branch of the local government council is headed by the chairman and assisted by a deputy. He is both the executive and the administrative officer of the council. His main function is to carry out policies set by the council and to ensure that local laws are enforced. The chairman who is the Chief Executive Officer of the council is basically in charge of the day-to-day operation of the council, including the supervision of all appointed officials and employees. The chairman is also in charge of hiring and firing all appointed officers and employees, subject to civil service rules. In general terms however, the chairman has authority to:

*   Enforce contracts
*   Preside over council meetings
*   Call special meetings of the council
*   Prepare a proposed budget
*   Report to council on the financial and other affairs and

needs of the council
* Perform as the ceremonial head of the council
* Approve and disapprove all official bonds

However, consistent with the separation of powers doctrine, the council is not authorized to interfere with the chairman's administration. Council members cannot give orders to departmental heads or other council employees. But for the council or legislative branch to do its job, it needs information on how the activity of the council operates. The chairman is the capable head in providing such information and this is where conflict comes in.

Feud over Policy

The law does not always spell out certain functions for the two organs. One frequent source of conflict is over personnel matters. Once the council is not happy with a chairman's appointment to a particular position or is dissatisfied with the performance of certain officers or employees, there is bound to be conflict between the two organs. On the other hand, when the executive branch believes that certain personnel policies interfere with their supervision of employees and hiring and firing of staff, conflict is bound to occur. In situations whereby the chairman directs all communications with the employees to go through his or her office, the council may feel that the chairman is dictating the stage and this can also lead to conflict.

Feud over Execution of Contracts

Looking at the functions of both organs in terms of contract, one can envisage clash of interest. While most of the contract agreements are entered into by the council or the legislative organ, the executive or chairman is to enforce the contract agreement. Conflict comes in when the contract bidding does not favour some members of the legislative branch or their subordinate associates. Most feuds in the local council are generated as a result of marginalization in award of contracts for the execution of certain projects in the local government council.

1. **Poor Funding and Poor Utilization of the Meager Funds:** The local government councils are poor financially. Whenever funds are released, both the executive and the legislative branch struggle for the control of such meager fund. In most cases spurious consultancies are created as veritable channels for siphoning the fund through close associates and loyalists.

2. **Poor Training Facilities:** Due to poor funding, training of personnel for a viable civil service structure is lacking. Facilities are either non-existent or inadequate. The result is invariably frustration and perfunctory performance. The aim of staff training and development becomes a non-issue since what would have been used for the training has been misappropriated. The result is high staff-turn-over without basic skills required to drive the local council affairs.

3. **Absence of Evaluation of Training Programmes:** The problem in the local government training extends to lack of evaluation process of the various training programmes carried out wherever such even exists. Evaluations always help to reveal lapses in the training programmes, especially between the personnel needs of the local government and the objective or contents of the training programmes, and between the trainees' career needs and the local government needs. If such evaluations are conducted periodically, it will enhance the quality of the content of the training programmes.

4. **Feud over the Independence of the Judiciary:** The judiciary, just like in the federal and state government structure, is the third branch of the local council. The role of the judiciary is to adjudicate on

the law passed by the legislature and implemented by the executive. Each of the three branches exercises certain defined role, free from unreasonable interference by the others. It is however realized that the executive branch of the council has more influence on the judiciary then the legislative. While the legislature strives hard to challenge this development, the executive continues to influence the judiciary in cases it has interest in. We must realize that the state government also checkmates the power of the local government chairman by appointing the judicial officers directly from the state judicial set-up.

Preventing and Resolving Executive–Legislative Conflict

It is essential for the Local Government Council members to understand their roles and how they relate to the roles of the chairman of the local government. Many conflicts in the local government areas are as a result of confusion as to these roles and the consequent overlapping of the boundaries between the respective branches. Although the boundaries in some cases may not be clearly stated, the basic roles of the chairman and councillors are derived from the basic structure of the state government.

The following strategies are suggested for creating an enabling environment for sustainable and conflict reduced collaboration between the Legislative and Executive branches in the Local Government system.

1. Establishment of Legislative-Executive Consultative Forum that will meet periodically to exchange views and ideas on the management of the local government system. This forum will create and sustain channels of communication between the two branches and clarify sticky points and grey areas.

2. Mutual Consultation is the key to conflict reduction. The Executive branch should endeavour to consult with

and carry the Legislature along in the execution of programmes and projects. Likewise the Legislature should also carry the Executive branch along while enacting bye-laws and exercising its oversight responsibilities. This will go a long way in reducing friction, building confidence, trust and goodwill.

3. Capacity building should be organized periodically for officials of both arms of government with a view of increasing their knowledge, competence and expertise in the management of local government affairs. This training programme will ensure that officials are familiar with their mandates and obligations, and will thus act in such a way and manner as to reduce conflict and friction.

4. A stakeholders' Forum should be established for quality input from community leaders. Members of the forum should be drawn from women, youth, religious, traditional, social and development structures and platforms. Such a forum is to act as an effective conflict prevention platform because it will always aggregate and respect the perspectives of different stakeholders, particularly the legislative and executive arms.

Conclusion

It is quite possible to build sustainable synergy between the executive and legislative arms at the local government level. This can be achieved through mutual collaboration, effective communication, striking of compromises, building of consensus and mutual respect. This positive process will have a salutary impact on local government administration and the empowerment of citizens who the local government was set up to serve in the first place.

Chapter

11

ON THE THRESHOLD OF PEACE AND
HARMONY: CONSTRUCTING AN MGBOWO
ELYSIUM IN AN ERA OF SOCIAL AND
CULTURAL CHANGE

Introduction

It is only proper that I begin this chapter with sincere
appreciation to the distinguished members of Klobb
Harmoni, Mgbowo Community for providing our people this
annual harvest of ideas during which a variant of this
discourse was presented. Such a platform as that is always
difficult to erect, and to all those, whose labour, courage
and vision have sustained this tradition, I give a million
thanks. I give this thanks because ideas rule the world, and
the art of transforming an environment by historical change
agents begins first as intimations of conscience driven by a
conscious application of the logic of reasoning, before it
encounters the wider social context of practice. By insisting
that we share ideas together, the members of this noble
association have truly affirmed the supremacy of intellectual
will and profound thought over the vulgar, and sometimes,
banal contradictions that define our social space.

151

As a then Director in a Presidential Institute charged with peace-building and conflict resolution, I was painfully aware of our lack of prompt intervention in containing the tragic eruption of mid-2006 in the community and incapacity in following up with the rigorous demands of post-conflict healing processes and reconstruction, both at the material and psychological planes.

Furthermore, I was troubled by the lack of sufficient intellectual distance between our people and the painful events and memories of the recent past; a deep emotional connection to the events that is capable of re-opening old wounds, inflaming latent passions and exhuming buried ghosts. Yet again, as a student of restorative justice, which finds exultation and rationalization in the ritual structure of African social healing paradigms, structures, mechanisms and strategies, I readily came to the conclusion that peace can only be built in a cathartic context; that is, it is only by purging ourselves of the hidden spring wells of fear, distrust and suspicion through a brutal exposition of the sources, character and shape of those tragic events that we can reconcile the differences within us, restore hope to a troubled land and re-humanize a traumatized people. The implication of this objective mindset is that harmony can only become an organic exemplification of our daily conduct and interaction on the strength of the attention we pay to the painful realities of our existence.

I have thus re-worked the initial topic of the original presentation to suit the temper of this book project. The chapter is now titled: "On the Threshold of Peace and Harmony: Constructing an Mgbowo Elysium in an Era of Social and Cultural Change." In making this change I am fully aware of its range, breadth and perspicacity, and if I succeed in pointing out the broad issues regarding the place of peace, harmony, culture and social practice in Mgbowo in this contemporary period of our historical evolution, I will feel satisfied that some sort of justice has been done to the subject matter at hand.

The Mythic Context

Any student of Classical Greek mythology knows that the mythic universe is broken or divided into three existential platforms: the **High Olympus** inhabited by the gods and goddesses that define the Greek pantheon, who structure the mythic world in such a way as to achieve order, peace and harmony for all life-forces; the **Upper Air**, or the world of matter, inhabited by men, beasts and plants, with the daily experiences of love, joy, torment, triumph, tragedy and despair; and **Hades,** or the **underworld,** wherein dead souls and spirits journey to as their final resting place, and which again is sub-categorized into the **Valley of Oblivion,** the **Infernal Regions** and **Elysium or Elysian Fields** or the **Plain of the Blessed**. The Valley of Oblivion is the incandescent region of transformation, a transitional – purgatory plane of judgement after which a soul departs either to the Infernal Regions of waste, disease, suffering, chaos, disorder, unending pain, lamentation or strife or to Elysium, a land of eternal bliss, peace, harmony, celestial joy, decorous behaviour and spiritual contentment.

The Mgbowo of today has become a metaphor of this classical mythic imagination. By examining the state of our culture and tradition; by examining the patterns of social relations; by underscoring the ingredients of spiritual, moral and ethical conducts; and by objectively situating recent historical events in the community in their proper context, we must come to the conclusion about whether our land today is either the Valley of Oblivion, the Infernal Regions of waste, suspicion, distrust, anarchy and spiritual aridity and inertia, or indeed the grove of the blessed, the Elysium of our collective dreams, anticipation and expectation.

Without a doubt, if the lessons of myth are anything to go by, Mgbowo has become an Infernal Region of visionless people led by elite who have lost their way, and who have systematically broken the dialogue and communion with our ancestors, our founding fathers and our heroes past. The umbilical cord that has always tied Mgbowo past to

Mgbowo present has been severed by this very elite who have left the people without leadership, without guidance, and without inspiration, trapped as they are, in a social and cultural wilderness they cannot master, and who repeatedly unleash the foul passions of discord, insensate anger, nauseating ambition and youth backlash on a hapless people.

While the community's legendary founders pursued the goal of creating a coherent social community bound by an intricate network of clan relationship and social, cultural and ritual institutions; and while they laboured gallantly to secure adequate space for the evolution of a common weal, which has the capacity of powering social transformation; while the heroes of educational advancement in the 1920s, 1930s, 1940s and 1950s, and the social and institution builders of the golden age of the 1970s and 1980s had nothing but unstinting love for the community, passionate commitment to its development and greatness, and invested intellect, time and material resources in pushing back the frontiers of ignorance, backwardness and superstition, the contemporary Mgbowo elite are only secure in their search for space to conquer and corrupt, and in sowing the seeds of discord and angst. And this is a process that has retarded social development, divided the people against themselves and created the condition in which we are now painfully searching for peace, harmony and social stability.

Historical Echoes

The present culture of unbelief in Mgbowo today may well be an exaggeration of the stresses and pressures imposed on the community by modernization with its fast-paced dialectics of social and cultural change, yet its symptoms are clearly deep-rooted in history. While it is true that the 1970s and 1980s was a period of accelerated social, political, cultural and economic transformation driven by a clear-sighted, visionary leadership, it also threw up centrifugal, divisive forces that are today destroying the institutional fabric of the community.

On the one hand, the period saw the rise of republican democracy entranced via the Community Council System and the Mgbowo Improvement Union, which articulated a people-based developmental needs and initiatives (expansion of the Central Community Market, construction of a town hall, resuscitation and equipping of dilapidated primary schools, the establishment of the Boys Secondary School and the two Girls Secondary and High Schools, etc). It also witnessed the emergence and rise of an articulate and dynamic leadership of the Church Council that commenced the building of the Catholic Pro-Cathedral and the Catholic Parish House, including a residential accommodation for the Parish Priest.

On the other hand, however, intra-elite rivalry which had always operated at a friendly level of competition and disputation, often times degenerated into open factionalization and collapse of elite consensus. The high point of this conscious disavowal of group consensus and solidarity was the chieftaincy selection process of about 1977 which split the town into two and eventually consequented in the factionalizaion of the MIU.

In a parenthetical sense, another major milestone of this period was the rise and emergence of several community based organizations and civic unions, age grade associations and women collectives, as well as well-structured, agenda-setting social groupings like the Klobb Harmoni and the Unique Organization among several others.

Thrown into the mix too was a vibrant and dynamic student association – HISSAM (Higher Institutions Student Association of Mgbowo)–which created tremendous impact in the area of youth mobilization for development and raising of youth consciousness in the area of political participation and mass empowerment – a tendency which was given an ideological tone by the Mass Consciousness Movement. However, a number of these structures and platforms were consumed by the intra-elite struggle for political power and operational space and have now become moribund – an omission that is also at the root of the crisis of identity and direction that has currently shackled the Mgbowo Community.

Interestingly, the historical echo which has successfully challenged the foundation of community-wide peace, harmony and political, social and cultural coherence has been the chieftaincy institution. An alien traditional platform which was originally crafted by the British hegemony at the turn of the last century to impose order on a captured populace was elevated in the mid-1970s by Col. Atom Kpera, Justice Agbakoba and Prof. G. N. Odenigwe in the whole of the then East-Central State as an affirmation of popular will. Apart from the factional in-fighting which trailed the selection of the first *Ohaire* of Mgbowo but which was contained and resolved over time, the new institution weakened the power base of the MIU, deconstructed the essence of participatory, people-led developmental initiatives propelled by the dismantled community council system and led to the emergence of a new class and structure of leadership that weighed heavily in favour of instant nobility with an illogical hierarchical structure.

Today, no community in Igboland has been able to successfully replace an Atom Kpera Chief, except in a few instances in which a new monied class, and most essentially, drug barons and conmen, have deployed unimaginable resources to bulldoze their way into such exalted traditional offices. The real problem is not even the ahistorical nature of these institutions which is a negation of the Igbo cosmological and cosmogenic character, but that the influence, power, splendour and respect they have garnered, the awe with which they are held, and the capacious space political administrations at the local, state and federal levels have opened up to them, mean an unending struggle for such offices, conspirational scheming, intra-elite contestation for power and ultimately, the collapse of social stability, peace and harmony.

Of course, I believe that these traditional institutions have a place in contemporary Mgbowo, nay Igbo environment, but their relevance must be balanced in relation to the institutional existence of other mass democratic civic and republican structures that exist in the land. It is precisely the incapacity of the elite to achieve this sense of balance that has led to the mismanagement of the "autonomy" question, the current factionalization of the MIU, the tragic events of July 2006, and the current search for amelioration, reconciliation and social, cultural and psychological restoration in the community.

Collapse of Elite Consensus

A major point worth examining in this discourse is the collapse of elite consensus in Mgbowo community. A town whose strength is anchored on group solidarity under a capable elite leadership, because of its relatively small size in relation to her neighbours, is today, at the political and traditional sectors, lacking of a leadership that commands universal respect and acceptability; that inspires and motivates the people; and is their rallying point in times of acute challenges, pressures and stresses. We have seen how elite consensus has suffered reversals of fortune in the past, but at no historical time has this phenomenon been as exaggerated and foregrounded as in the present time. Dialogue among the elite is conducted at the factional level, with motivations that are less than pious, sublime and noble, driven as these dialogues are by a narrow-minded world view, insipient ambition and banal sentiments.

The MIU remains a shadow of its once towering self-image, riddled by division and incapacitated by lack of a coherent vision that can re-empower the people driven to despair by lack of social and political direction. If consensus among the elite had not collapsed, so much space wouldn't have been conceded to the forces that unleashed the mayhem of 2006, on both sides. If elite consensus did not collapse, the challenges posed by the autonomous community dialectic in relation to a unified, centralized Mgbowo identity would have been handled with maturity, tact, common sense and sound logic because it is quite possible, and even practicable, that the two realities can coexist, mutually reinforcing one another at different levels of articulation and performance.

The history of social transformation the world over, including revolutionary transformations, is the history of elite mobilization, and the mobilization of other social classes by the elite so mobilized. As change agents, the elite are the engine of history, powering advancement and giant strides, galvanizing human and material resources for quantum developmental leaps, and providing vision, leadership and direction to the rest of society. Whether as guardians of sacred institutions, or as political and administrative heads of civic unions; whether as custodians of tradition and culture expressed in their various institutions and platforms; or as members of the intelligentsia or successful merchants, they erect the sustainable structures that drive society, and conduct themselves in such a manner as to inspire their generation.

I address the issue of peace and harmony with tragedy as its backdrop because the Mgbowo elite have failed the community in action, and in words. They have, as I stated elsewhere, broken the dialogue with our ancestors, and disconnected the past from the present. If this judgment appears harsh, and is even directed at myself too, it is as it should be, because to move Mgbowo forward, we must be objective, brutal and thorough in our analysis. We must be self-critical in our assessment of the current problems in our midst and must be ready to accept the collective censure of the mass of the people who look up to the elite for leadership but who are constantly betrayed by what the renowned Pan-Africanist, Frantz Fanon described thus:

> The future will have no pity for those who having the exceptional privilege of speaking words of truth to the oppressors, have instead taken refuge in an attitude of passivity, mute indifference, and sometimes of cold complicity.

In a related context the same Fanon opined that, "every generation must, out of relative obscurity, discover its mission, betray it or fulfill it". Sadly, and most tragically, the present generation of Mgbowo elite still wallows in obscurity and have not even discovered their identity and mission, not to talk of betraying or fulfilling it.

Generational Disconnect

Social scientists, particularly sociologists, are quick to point out that a key ingredient of positive social transformation and social stability is sustainable dialogue and communication across generational lines. The idea of generational connection is thus at the heart of social coherence without which a community instantly loses its way, and is periodically engulfed by one form of conflict, sometimes of a violent and disruptive nature, or the other.

Presently, there is very minimal positive communication between the elders and the youths of Mgbowo. Existing contexts, patterns and character of any ongoing connection is defined by raw aggression, structures of usage, intimidation, rebelliousness and irreconcilable differences. Significant portions of the youth elements are alienated from mainstream cultural, social, economic and political discourses and processes, with the implication that their passions, repressed ideas and standpoints on issues find expression in anti-social, violent activities. Added to this situation is the dysfunctional nature of community-wide social relationships which are structured in favour of self-promoting and self-aggrandizing pyrotechnics. The elite who harbour this mindset only see the youth as willing tools to deploy to effectuate their perfidious agendas. Lacking the capacity for independent thought and intellectual depth; and without a powerful, goal-driven youth assembly that can rally them around a noble banner, these youth elements accept their marginal, alienated existence and find meaning in reckless acts that further undermine the community's sense of purpose and meaning.

Generational disconnect in Mgbowo thus operates at different levels: the disconnect between the living past and the present it rationalizes, reinforces and animates; the disconnect between the ideas of the present day elite leadership and the patriotic sacrifices of the community's founding fathers and heroes past; and the broken dialogues across the presently existing generational lines. Given this concrete scenario, it is not surprising that Mgbowo is currently witnessing retarded social and cultural development; is a safe haven for all manners of undesirable elements; and has experienced a volatile period of destructive conflict with the attendant loss of lives and properties – a process that is anathema to the spiritual, mythic and ritual paradigms of the town's origins and sources and which may require a sustained period of cleansing before order, coherence and stability could be re-established.

Crisis of Social and Cultural Transformation

Social and cultural transformation is an integral part of the law of natural succession. Changes in value-system, attitude, perception of reality and traditional practices are driven by the forces of modernization and political and economic development. An essential element of the dialectics of nature is the view that man changes and transforms nature, and in that process changes and transforms himself. In effect, no community stands still; it must, sooner than later, become overwhelmed by the laws and forces of change, and in so doing begins to incarnate the values, beliefs and attitudes such changes engender. Mgbowo community, like every other community, has been fundamentally transformed over an immense historical time, from its traditional moorings into a modern environment. This modernity is to be seen in the architectural design of the houses, in the pursuit of Western education and the job opportunities and wealth it creates, in new economic enterprises and business ventures, in the people's style of dressing, and in the appreciation of music and other creative products of culture.

However, social and cultural transformation is a complex and complicated process. The struggle to replace an old way of thinking and acting creates levels of social and cultural dislocations which have the capacity of disrupting social stability, peace and harmony. Particularly, among the youth, the release of excess energy in various directions could become violent in nature, and readily leads to conflict between them and their parents and the older members of the community who still cling, somewhat tenuously, to the old value-systems.

Every community must therefore establish, reinforce, nurse and sustain institutions and platforms which have the capacity of achieving balance, peace, harmony and decorous conduct in time of change. It must have a strong and coherent political and administrative structure that coordinates social activities and processes, and that inspires the people on channeling their energies to worthy and noble social causes. It must also have a dynamic traditional institution that bridges past cultural practices with modern cultural attitudes, while at the same time developing and deploying traditional mechanisms and strategies of conflict resolution on which is anchored the social and cultural health and well-being of such a community.

We have demonstrated in the preceding part of this discourse that Mgbowo community is currently devoid of such institutions of mass mobilization and mass participation in the burning issues of the day. With a political and administrative set up that is frozen in time, inept and wracked by factionalization; and with a disordered and disorganized traditional institution that has polarized the community and bred distrust, enmity and ravanchist mentality among the elite, the process of social transformation in Mgbowo has become an atavistic process of collective immolation and cultural dissonance.

As things stand today, chaos and disorder best describe the Mgbowo social and cultural reality. The town is without electricity because social miscreants have vandalized power lines and other assets as far back as 1991 or 1992. The Mgbowo section of the highway between Enugu and Port Harcourt is the most dangerous segment of the road, controlled by highway robbers who maim, steal and defile passengers at will. The town currently hosts assorted criminal gangs who have parceled off large swatches of its territory as a no go area; indeed as their secure base and haven of plotting unimaginable evil. Prostitution, drug abuse, social licentiousness, anarchic social conducts, violent behaviour, and unwanted pregnancies clearly define the town's social space. Without a powerful, goal-driven and agenda-setting youth assembly to impose order and discipline and ennoble the young with patriotic acts, passion and sentiment, the army of unemployed youth roam the streets and pathways aimlessly, completely distantiated and alienated from mainstream productive economic, political and social ventures.

However, the youth do not share this blame alone. No articulate, community-wide effort has been made to re-construct, re-educate, re-socialize and empower them. With generational disconnect as the haunting spectre of Mgbowo social experience, the elite find themselves ensconced in their fortified dwelling places, and have abandoned other available spaces for hordes of uninspired youths to occupy. In essence, the structure, pattern and character of social and cultural transformation in Mgbowo is a clear and present danger to the community's peaceful and harmonious foundation and existence and a daunting challenge that will require vigorous action and deep intellectual and strategic thought to put right.

The Recent Historical Tragedy

In early July, 2006, a tragedy of indescribable magnitude befell Mgbowo community. It left a trail of death and destruction of property, shattered and traumatized lives, broke relationships, tore families and friends apart and caused to set in a season of cultural anomie, angst, unbelief and shock. While the immediate cause may well have been the contestation for traditional power, influence and authority among different factions of the elite; and while it may have drawn strength and impetus from the crisis in the MIU and contradictions in a number of villages that make up the community where local discord had previously assumed a violent dimension, yet the sources of that tragedy was embedded in a longer spatial-temporal cycle. We have already described the historical and social sources of that tragedy, and only the very myopic would characterize it as a consequence of an immediate situation.

The scale on which that tragedy deconstructed and attenuated peace, harmony, social stability and cordial relationship among people and entities is a harsh lesson to us all about the excess of passion and ambition, and an admonition that narrow selfish interests and vainglorious pride among all the disputants can lead to nothing but pain. A mediation process is required which is capable of restoring hope, healing wounds and reconstructing relationships as a prelude to restoring psychic harmony to a violated land. This, of course, is the concrete challenge of the moment; the reconciliation of differences, the acceptance of inadequacies and blame, and a community-wide rite of purification and ritual passage that can connect a bastardized present to its glorious past.

The Search for Peace and Harmony

Like all conflict-prone communities, the search for peace and harmony in Mgbowo will be a long and difficult one. The peace building agenda and post-conflict reconstruction strategies are never a single event or even a series of loosely connected events. It is a process and processes are difficult to attain, master and sustain. Some of the guidelines that should be focused on in the course of mediation, reconciliation and restoration of harmony include:

i.   An objective assessment of immediate and remote

       sources and causes of discord in the community

ii.   A clear determination of actors and interests that shape and drive conflict in the community

iii. An examination of the clear lack of capacity by the MIU to provide effective political leadership in Mgbowo

iv. An examination of the place of traditional institution in Mgbowo in the context of the autonomous vs. Mgbowo-as-one divide/dialectic

v.   An examination of the social, cultural and economic setting of Mgbowo, with particular reference to the place of the youth in wealth-creation and social transformation.

Some specific issues that need close attention with regard to the Mgbowo peace process are:

i.   Setting up a community-wide, all inclusive peace and reconciliation committee that will draw its membership from all stakeholders, interest groups, factions, civic unions, women associations and youth groups.

ii.   Systematically working towards the withdrawal of all subsisting court cases, as the judicial process can never produce a win-win situation.

iii. Setting up of a think tank that will take a fresh look at the Mgbowo traditional institutions, and establish a workable relationship and balance between the prerogatives of Mgbowo-as-one and the emergent reality of the autonomy phenomenon.

iv. Convening an all-delegates MIU conference that will have in attendance all branches and tendencies within the group, and re-empowering its institutional and administrative structure and mechanism for proper service delivery.

v.   Declaring a week of peace and harmony in Mgbowo which will involve a series of healing activities that will culminate in an Mgbowo peace rally.

As sketchy as these ideas are, they are a good starting point in the search of peace and harmony in the community. If anything, the essential rationalization of this kind of discourse is to generate dialogue and debate, to provoke discussion and to break the stifling silence of the graveyard which has descended on the town.

Conclusion: Mgbowo on the Threshold of a New Elysium

The search for Elysium is the eternal yearning of all mankind. The struggle for humanization of peoples and societies is designed to overcome existential fear and despair. Castles of peace and harmony are only constructed by the courage and will of men and women who defy the boundaries of social myopia so as to embrace the calming elixir of noble passions. The Mgbowo Elysium is not merely a dream, a longing for lost paradise, but an idea and reality whose time has come. Indeed, out of the despairing nuances of present day social discord and strife can emerge a new world of hope and love. But this must be worked for, with matchless commitment and uncommon courage. In the end, Mgbowo is the only gift that we have, a gift we must cherish and nurture to perfection, as humanly as this is possible. We must thus conquer the demons of division and fractionalization, still the dark spirits of anger, rancour and bitterness and begin the required process of reconciling ourselves to ourselves, men, women and children who love Mgbowo and are prepared to repair and reconnect the broken communal umbilicus to the ancestral navel of our distant beginning.

Chapter

12

THE RELEVANCE OF THE HUMANITIES IN A TECHNOLOGY-DRIVEN WORLD

Introduction

This subject matter of this chapter which grew out of a presentation I made to the Faculty of Humanities of University of Abuja occupies a special place in my heart for after a fairly long period of absence and disconnection, I am truly back among kindred spirits, the genuine guardians of the sacred word. The sacredness of the humanities is self-evident in their ennoblement of the human condition and in directing the compass of human consciousness. I made the choice to be here and to share my thoughts with you, consciously and deliberately, because I believe in my heart that I am a humanist, ever was and ever shall be.

This deliberate choice was long made when as a High School Senior I chose English and Literary Studies and Philosophy and Religious Studies (in that order) as my preferred university disciplinary choices over others. Before I left high school and proceeded to the university to study English and Literature I had consumed the classics of literature, philosophy and history. And for 10 years (1988-1998) I taught Literature and researched into Igbo studies as a university teacher, putting out a substantial body of scholarly works as a testament of my commitment, fidelity and passion to the humanities. Yet, the past eight or so years (1998-2008), has seen me veer off in another trajectory, attempting, as it were, to create a balance between the pursuit of knowledge and intellect and social practice in the area of human rights, democratic struggle and institution building, and finally peace studies. I have, inevitably become significantly distantiated from my humanistic rooting and substantially discontinued rigorous, vigorous and profound intellectual, scholarly and research pursuits. I have, before my very eyes, become one of humanities prodigal children, caught between the exhilarating world of Faculty room debates and discourses and the complicated reality of social engagements.

As Chinweizu *et al* admonished a generation of Eurocentric artists and scholars in a controversial 1973 article that gave birth to the greater controversy that *Toward the Decolonization of African Literature* became in 1980, I have been persuaded to come home from intellectual exile to the welcoming embrace of the "in-crowd". This reconnection to the cause of the humanities is a special kind of homecoming for me, a re-engagement with the ideals that the humanities stand firm to uphold and protect, and a fervent hope that they can successfully bridge the distances between intellectual conscience and social practice. To embrace the welcoming atmosphere provided by the foregathered kindred spirits is to take back life from the haunting depths of social Golgotha which our nation has descended into and become and to be purified by the healing balm of the humanities' Elysian peace after a persistent sojourn in society's Valley of Oblivion.

Through a series of reflection, by far not a well made presentation, it is my intention to seduce us all to the humanities' free spirit, its sense of accommodation and tolerance. As our society becomes transfigured by the winds of technological change and its various advertisements, the humanities must reclaim the lost ground and disused space they presently occupy; and must reassert its vitality and viability, its meaning and essence, its significance and durability. It is my claim that the humanities must remain faithful to its pristine ideals, unyielding in its commitment to truth and obligations to wider social publics, while at the same time renewing its spirit to accommodate the challenges posed by a vastly changed and changing time.

To bridge the distances I alluded to will require thematic adaptation and response to a technology-driven world not in an effort to create a being with debilitating congenital abnormalities, a half mutant of two worlds, but by harnessing the finest traditions of the humanities in mastering and overcoming the challenges posed by everyday living. This is precisely where I believe the humanities stand today in Nigeria: a relentless pursuit of knowledge and wisdom not for their sake alone, but as a transformative idiomatic properties of change and social renewal in such a way and context as to restore honour to an ancient heritage while at the same time mounting a resolute battle against the rage of social parasitism and cultural imbecility.

This conference couldn't have been coming at a more auspicious time considering that our age is characterized by:

- Crisis of identity and consciousness;
- Crisis of values and culture;
- Crisis of underdevelopment, particularly poverty; and
- Crisis of governance.

Humanities must thus surmount the odds and obstacles they presently face and rise to the challenges of national development.

Context of Definition

From the conference call for papers, we can begin to appreciate the range and diversity of the disciplinary discourses that fall under the humanities:

- Language and linguistics;
- Literature;
- Theatre Arts;
- History;
- Philosophy;
- Religion;
- Media studies; and
- Archival studies (archeology), record storage, etc.

As incomplete as this list appears, it gives a healthy insight into the integral, multi-disciplinary framework that defines the humanities, and the nexus they establish with such other cogent issues as:

- Gender discourse and women empowerment;
- Paradigm shifts in national development;
- The Human situation; unity and national survival;
- Democracy, good governance, rule of law; and
- Technological development.

Essence

It would appear axiomatic that the essential thrust of all humanities is the placement of man, and by extension, humanity at the centre of academic enquiry and intellectual discourse; the total pursuit, investigation and interrogation of the human condition; the scrutiny of man as a carrier of culture, civilization and values in a successive order of historical progression; and emphasis on humanism as a derivative, epistemological category that allows for empathy, compassion, sensitivity and tolerance in the study of man, including all his foibles and failures, successes and triumphs.

Dominant Challenges

The primary challenge that faces the humanities is the continual declaration of their relevance in a technology-driven world. This will task to the maximum the mental, academic and intellectual resources of all practitioners given the relentless assault on the foundation of their integrity by an anti-intellectual, de-academicized social and political environment, even at the highest level of the polity.

- By the pitiless war waged on human cultural values and essences by an anti-cultural military establishment that dominated statecraft for upwards of 30 + years in Nigeria's 48 years of nationhood;
- By the grip of a globalized world order that trumpets all manners of technocratic and techno-scientific advertisements;
- By the internet, www and ICT age and their various forms of applications; and
- By the retreat of ideology, especially its Marxist variant, from the mainstream global intellectual exchange where arguably the majority of Nigerian and African scholars who share these notions are to be found in the humanities and the social sciences.

The struggle thus has been a desperate reach for relevance and accommodation in an environment that is pushing the pursuit of science and all its associated fields to the limit. This search has taken such radical paths as the outright scraping of several humanities disciplines in some universities; and the re-conceptualization and the redefinition of titles of other disciplines to accommodate the "requirements" of our contemporary age.

The second main challenge is the problematic of striking a balance and bridging the distance between the specificities of the humanities as academic disciplines, and an intellectual vocation, and their adaptation and domestication to suit the current economic, social and technological challenges that face the nation. Rephrased somewhat, the implication of this is as follows:

Should we, as exponents of the finest tradition of man's eternal search for signification and meaning, in an increasingly complex world, continue to thunder down from the mountain top of academia to the din and clatter of daily struggle at the valley of existence, expounding new truths and sometimes iconoclastic values that "time but tries its teeth in vain" to use Nietzsche's expression, whether we are heard or understood or not, or should we abandon our intellectual conscience and academic integrity and align our pursuits to the mundane realities of existence, even if this unleashes untold violence to our calling?

If not, how can we achieve that balance between intellectual fidelity and social practice; between academic discourse and social and economic imperatives; and between ideas in their pristine form and the demands of national development? I believe that the resolution of this challenge is key to the future of the humanities in Nigeria, and through that, the resolution of the crisis of national development. I believe that this national conference is a good starting point in this dialogue, in this interrogation of the meaning, essence and significance of the humanities in our search for prosperity and common good. Given the range of themes being examined.

National Development

What then are the ingredients of national development to which the humanities are called upon to respond to? Nigerian development is aligned, in a globalized world, to the challenges already universally identified by the UN. These are the 8 Millennium Development Goals that emphasize the primacy of human infrastructure and human security in social transformative processes. Continentally, this is aligned to the New Partnership for African Development (NEPAD) whose essence is defined:

•   By building of partnerships across multi-layered sectors;

- Good governance;
- Poverty reduction;
- Collective security and defence;
- Mechanism for conflict prevention, management and resolution;
- Human capital development; and
- National assets (Preservation and restoration).

Nationally, the primary driving platform for social and economic transformation is the NEEDS I and II documents, again, with emphasis on poverty reduction through wealth creation; building of partnerships; private sector driven, free market economy; infrastructural renewal; and regime of good governance, accountability, probity, transparency, due process, service compact etc.

It is not my responsibility to examine the direct correlation between the humanities and these indices of national development in response to the challenges already identified, but to provide broad strokes on certain general directions that the humanities may and can take in the area of social practice.

- Language as a carrier of cultural values and identity must engage issues pertaining to indigenous languages, orthographies, publishing in indigenous language, children and indigenous language.
- Literature must respond to the demands of indigenous literature, orature, literature of social commitment and social action, critical scholarship that establishes connection between aesthetics and social and political practice, and the evolution of truly authentic African aesthetics that responds to the social issues of our time.
- History – connecting the past to the future with the present as a backdrop; history and social experience and social reality; history and democratic tradition and consolidation; profound investigation of community history and collective memory.
- Theatre Arts – seems to have taken the lead with the

emergence of home videos, commercial potentials of popular community theatre; drama in the aid of national causes: unity, conflict resolution, peace building, etc.

- Philosophy–the mother of all knowledge and the cradle of the humanities, may begin to shed some of its esoteric aura in favour of the practical application of philosophic truths to social and economic needs; development of indigenous philosophic modes that bear directly on people's needs, etc.
- Archeology–restoration and preservation of national assets; discoveries that aid the explication of common heritage and equally uncommon diversities; relating the past to the present through excavation of collective remembrances, etc.
- Religion–national unity, inter-faith understanding, culture of dialogue and tolerance, ecumenism, mankind's common spiritual heritage, etc.

The Humanities and the Culture of Dependency

Our humanities and social sciences must liberate themselves from a stifling culture of dependency to the so-called mainstream Western intellectual and theoretical canons by becoming increasingly proactive and interventionist in search for order and coherence in our world. They must draw from the liberationist paradigm of Ngugi wa Thiong'o in *Moving the Centre;* from Edward Said in *Orientalism, Culture and Dependency* and the *Representations of the Intellectual;* from the works of Cheick Anta Diop, Homi Bhabha, Gayatri Chakravorty Spivak, Aijaz Ahmad, and as troubling as it is, from Ali Mazrui's concept of the *Triple Heritage.*

Our scholars must engage the generation-defining ideas of the likes of Francis Fukuyama in the *End of History and the Last Man;* Paul Kennedy in the *Rise and Fall of the Great Powers* and *Preparing for the 21st Century;* Samuel Huntington in the *Clash of Civilizations and Remaking of the*

World Order and John Lukacs in *The End of the 20th Century
and the End of the Modern Age,* among numerous such other
works. Intellectual boldness, originality, vision and rigour,
and with an eye on the great developmental issues and
debates of our time, shall define our conduct and celebrate
our presence.

A Cautionary Note

Yet, before we are carried away, let us come down to earth
and recognize that the greatest of all challenges is that of
national poverty which has reduced a great number of our
people to the continual, perpetual and unceasing struggle
for existence. For as Will Durant puts it: "It is only in the
condition of wealth and leisure that the space can open up
for us to share ideas, to make timeless declarations and to
thunder from the mountain top. And only in this context
can our society and its rulers spare us the charge of
irrelevance and allow us to do what we know how best to
do; to generate ideas, to re-define value and meaning, to
create essence for things and people, and to make statements
that will still find worthy significance in generations, or even
millennia to come". In the same words of Durant, originally
addressed to an American audience but which resonate
powerfully in our clime today:

> It becomes evident that our ancient dependence on
> European thought is lessening, that we are beginning
> to do our own work in philosophy, literature, and
> science, and in our own way... but if we find it hard
> to surpass ourselves, and are sometimes discouraged
> with our own superficiality, our provincialism, our
> narrowness, our immature intolerance and our timid
> violence against innovation and experiment – let us
> remember that England needed eight hundred years
> between her foundation and her Shakespeare; and
> that France needed eight hundred years between her
> foundation and her Montaigne. We are drawn to us
> from Europe, and selected for survival an imitation

among ourselves, rather the initiative individualist and the acquisitive pioneer than the meditative and artistic souls; we have had to spend our energies in clearing our great forests and tapping the wealth of our soil; we have had no time yet to bring forth a native literature and a mature philosophy. But we have become wealthy, and wealth is the prelude to art. In every country where centuries of physical effort have accumulated the means for luxury and leisure, culture has followed as naturally as vegetation grows in a rich and watered soil. To have become wealthy was the first necessity; and people too must live before they can philosophize. No doubt we have grown faster than nations usually have grown; and the disorder of our souls is due to the rapidity of our development. We are like youth disturbed and unbalanced, for a time, by the sudden growth and experiences of puberty. But soon our maturity will come; our minds will catch up with our bodies, our culture with our possessions. Perhaps there are greater souls than Shakespeare's and greater minds than Plato's waiting to be born. When we have learned to reverence liberty as well as wealth, we too shall have our Renaissance.

(Will Durant, *The Story of Philosophy,* New York, Washington Square Press, preface).

Conclusion

The harsh lesson from the above long quotation from Will Durant's *The Story of Philosophy* is a poignant one: the transition from invention to prosperity, penury to wealth, underdevelopment to technological attainment; and with this a transition in belief systems, values and precepts is humanities' burden of being and proof. When should creative and other intellectual pursuits occur? By allowing our society significant space for the dawning of science and technology, modernity and development, or by engendering this possibility through the intervention of the humanities? What is the proper meeting point between culture and science, art and technology, drama and communication?

These questions find no easy or ready answers. Individually, we can stake our claim to social relevance by what we do, while collectively we must begin empowering the humanities with the capacity of breaking down some of its insular values, its inward gazing nature, in order to achieve the balance we have already declared is possible for them to attain; the balance between genuine disciplinary demands and the necessity of logical involvement in social practice.

To achieve this balance, and through that, to bridge social and intellectual distances, will create a new generation of humanists who, while honouring the egregious foundation of knowledge, will also celebrate the builders of the nation-state, with their accumulated knowledge and wide learning. I believe that this new attitude will not remain a dream for long but a reality we are already dwelling in as the various exponents of the humanities engage in the complex labour of helping our society find its lost way, re-discover it, reason and overcome its developmental maladies.

Chapter

13

THE PHANTOM, HIS OPERA AND CULTURAL OBSCURANTISM IN NIGERIA: A REFLECTION

Introduction

My journey towards a deep understanding, appreciation and enthusiastic acceptance of the cultural value of classical music, operatic music, serious music and crossover music – the last category will include the music of Enya, Vangelis, Enigma, Adiemus and Era – is symptomatic of the limit-situation problematic that define, and even over-determine, cultural awareness and recognition by the individual and society in Nigeria. Indeed, the challenge of being aware, and thus recognizing universal cultural expression in music as a source and carrier of universal values, ideas and knowledge has engendered a crisis of cultural consciousness as a national cultural trait. Cultural incoherence, and ultimately distantiation and dissociation, affect both the elite with a relatively high degree of individual cultural exposure – pertinently still unharnessed for a wider consumption – and the mass of the people whose grossly limited musical experience remains essentially kitsch.

I first "stumbled" into a serious appreciation of classical music upon visiting Rev. (Fr.) Prof. Jude Aguwa at Okigwe in 1989 and being subjected, so I thought then, to a quantum auditory punishment for a musical expression that was apparently lacking in rhythm, discernible structure and high points of luscious declaration. Prior to this encounter, my only other exposure to this genre of music was by listening to Pete Edochie's presentation of "Music from the Masters" on ABC in the early and mid-1980s, without paying any close attention to his narration on the composers, selected music, date of composition, universal meaning and significance, etc.

Seeing Fr. Aguwa's absorption with the music, the radiance on his face and an overwhelming feeling of spiritual contentment and peace, convinced me about the necessity of sharing this experience. To enforce my new will and realize my ambition, as it were, of being a connoisseur, I not only borrowed and recorded his audio tapes that filled a carton, but proceeded to lock up all my Rock and Roll tapes (oldies, hard and metallic) inside a drawer and made sure that I never went near the key for upwards of a year! My first random, haphazard and unstructured approach to classical music led me progressively into a strange, bewildering but increasingly revealing and profoundly rewarding world of Handel, Mozart, Beethoven, Wagner, Chopin, Bach and Tchaikovsky.

In 1990, I got my first introduction to operatic music in a video cassette recording of the "Three Tenors in Concert" for the soccer world cup of that year, which was staged in Italy. Arthur Nwankwo had brought the tape back from London and we would spend countless hours immersed in the vocal range, dramatic power and sheer elegance and splendour of that exuberant celebration of song, poetry and music conducted by the indomitable maestro – Zubin Mehta. Between 1990 and 1998 when I had recorded and watched the repeat performances by the Three Tenors in Los Angeles, USA (1994 World Cup) and Paris, France (1998 World Cup), got hold of various recordings of the Three Tenors on Tour, a recording of Luciano Pavarotti's performance at Hyde Park in 1991, Jessye Norman Sings *Carmen* and various other video cassettes of Opera Favourites, I deepened my knowledge of the genre, absorbed the elemental and enigmatic cultural force behind operatic compositions and got exposed to a totally different form of dramatic literature, yet connected somewhat to the dramaturgical qualities of total theatre, dance-drama and pantomimic representation, which I studied as a student of drama and literature.

Influential at this stage in the development of my classical music consciousness were two audio cassette tapes given me by my friend and research collaborator, Kurt Thometz at Brooklyn, New York in July, 1997, which contained the recording of Maria Callas's, etc performance of Acts One and Two of *TOSCA* and portions of Berlioz's *Damnation of Faust,* Bizet's *Carmen* and Donizetti's *Lucia di Lammermoor.* I was also impressed and influenced by the renditions, as soundtracks, of classical songs and arias, in a number of popular films, which I enjoyed watching then, like *Fatal Attraction* (*Madama Butterfly*) *Witches of Eastwick* (*Mozart and Beethoven*) and *Original Sin* (**"La Donna e Mobile"**).

I even engaged in lively debates about who is the greatest of the Three Tenors. While I adored Pavarotti and became his unabashed fan and devotee, because of his "heroic brilliance", vocal range, suppleness, purity and clarity of voice and tone, and sheer stage presence, Arthur Nwankwo held up Placido Domingo as the better singer on account of his dramatic ability and intensity and the classical and royal effect he brings on stage. Yet, we appreciated Jose Carreras' passionate and romantic appeal, the delicacy of his voice and his sacrifice and commitment to operatic music in spite of the life-threatening ailment he suffered.

Today, I have the major performances of Pavarotti, Domingo and Carreras on CD, cassette tape and DVD, apart from assembling an impressive collection of the works of all the leading classical composers. I have played, on CD, the complete version of Bizet's *Carmen,* Berlioz's *The Damnation of Faust* and Delibe's *Lakme* (particularly "The Flower Duet"), among tens of other operas, as well as enriching my library with the works of the Italian **bel canto** composers like Bellini, Vincenzo and Donizetti; the immortal creations of the romanticists like Verdi (*Rigoletto, La Traviata, Aida, Travatore and Othello*), and *Puccini* (*La Boheme, Tosca, Madama Butterfly, La Fanciulla Del West, La Rondine* and the incomplete *Turandot* – his only work written in the impressionistic style); and the anti-Wagner and anti-romanticist Ruggero Leoncavallo (*Paglliaci and Cavalleria Rusticana*) who substituted the quasi-historical romantic storyline with sensational stories from everyday life.

Carmen's "Prelude" and "Habanera", "Chorus of the Hebrew Slaves", "La Donna e Mobile", "E Lucevan le Stelle", "Vesti la gubba", "Donna mon vidi mai", and of course "Nessun Dorma" and "Conte Patiro", the two anthems of opera, find as much space as the works of Fela, Michael Jackson, the pop music culture in Nigeria up to the early 1980s, Little Richard, Paul Simon, Bob Dylan, The Rolling Stones, Bad Company, Boston, Carlos Santana, Bob Marley, AC/DC, and the modern country singers like Garth Brooks, Colin Raye and Billy Ray Cyrus, in my daily repertoire of songs and music to be played and enjoyed, over and over again. It is worth noting too that I have on CD and DVD the recordings of performances of popular arias from Caruso to Andrea Boceli, and from Maria Callas to Sarah Brightman with Angela Gheorghiu, Renee' Fleming, Amaury Vassili, Rolando Villazon, Anna Netbreko, Bryn Terfel, Juan Florez Diego, Noah Stewart, Jackie Evancho, Katherine Jenkins, Harley Westernra, Josh Grobhan, Russell Watson, Joan Sutherland and Kiri Te Kanawa and, literally speaking, the works of tens of other leading tenors and sopranos in between them.

Sometime in 1997, I got hold of a CD recording of various composers, artistes and musicians. On playing it, I was profoundly moved by a track called "The music of the night".

The composer was unknown to me, and great portions of the lyrics were lost to me given the classical technique of singing, but I felt I was in the presence of something totally unique, eternal and ethereal that possessed the soul and sub-consciousness with effortless ease and a powerful, vice-like grip.

I duly made a recording of that song in a cassette tape that contained the whole songs in *Evita* (as of then I was unaware of who *Evita's* composer was) and Michael Jackson's "Earthsong". Believe it or not, I was to play "The Music of the Night" a thousand times over, literally speaking, between 1997 and 2004 without as yet ever hearing the name of Andrew Lloyd Webber or even associating him as the composer of that music, even though I had watched *Jesus Christ Superstar* during my undergraduate days at University of Nigeria Nsukka (UNN) (again, without knowing who composed it!).

Sometime in 2004 or 2005 I watched on the CNN or Sky News a preview of the film version of *The Phantom of the Opera,* composed by Andrew Lloyd Webber, during which snatches of several songs, including "The Music of the Night" were played. This was the first time I would associate the song with Lloyd Webber and *The Phantom of the Opera.* I set out to purchase the film in a small video shop. The copy I bought must have been a pirated one, poorly recorded, with hazy shadows over it, and not playing particularly well. Yet, I played it over and over again, hoping that one day I would come across a really great copy of the film. That wish has been more than fulfilled for I now have 5 authentic copies of the film, purchased during my visits to Australia, New Zealand, South Africa, England and the USA, and at the Nu Metro Media Stores in Abuja, Nigeria.

I got five copies because two of them could not play on my PC because of regional coding. In addition, I also have now in my collection, Andrew Lloyd Webber's *Cats, Evita, Requiem,* Joseph and the Techni-Colour Dream Coat and *Jesus Christ Superstar* (all on DVD), as well as "Andrew Lloyd

Webber's Masterpiece" (live performance of his musicals in
The People's Republic of China in both DVD and CD), "The
Magical Music of Andrew Lloyd Webber" (3 CD box set),
"Simply Musicals" and "Simply Soundtracks" (4 CD box set
collection each, containing his major compositions), "Sarah
Brightman in Concert", a DVD that contains selections from
Webbers musicals, plus the enchanting and celebratory "Con
te Patiro)" and another CD titled "Highlights from The
Phantom of the Opera".

For several nights of late, I have watched *The Phantom of
the Opera,* in between the writing of a three volume work
on my intellectual development and social practice, and as
I studied the film closely (I have read the lyrics from the
booklet inside a two CD box set of its original recording, which
I purchased in Maryland, USA in 2005), I started reflecting
on the deeper meaning of the musical and its implications
for Nigeria's awareness of its cultural being, and the challenges
strewn along the path of its self-recovery by dark, brooding
and atavistic political and cultural forces. It is this reflection
that prompted this essay, and provided me with the inspiration
and energy to put my thoughts down.

I must confess that I have not read a single line of any
review or critical commentary on either the stage musical
or its cinematic version. This situation has its advantage
and disadvantage. It has given me the freedom to explore
my thoughts and pursue my reflection as I deem it fit,
without being encumbered or over burdened by recourse to
what others have written. It is thus possible that, freed from
a cross-textual comparative analysis, my reflection, while
not being original, would at least be fresh, creatively and
uniquely mine. On the other hand, this lack of critical
exposure has the capacity of limiting the range, scope and
dimension of my analysis in not tapping into the rich
resources of available critical assessment of the subject. I
settled for the first option.

The Phantom of the Opera is a cinematic adaptation of
the stage musical composed by Andrew Lloyd Webber, and

which in turn is based on *Le Fantome De L'Opera*, a gothic novel of heightened reality and soaring tragic romance, written by the late 19th century-early 20th century French novelist, Gaston Leroux, who was born in 1868. The novel, which was his greatest, was published in 1911. Between its publication and 2004, it had been adapted into Cinema and Television ten times, a testimony to its archetypal essence and universal appeal. Historically, the first film version was in 1925, the second in 1943, the third in 1962, the fourth in 1983, as well as a Television version in 1990. Andrew Lloyd Webber's stage version won the Laurence Olivier and *Evening Standard* award for best musical when it opened in London in 1986. During the intervening years, it has also won over seventeen major theatre awards in 22 countries, been performed over 7,000 times in nearly 120 cities around the world and has been watched by about 100 million people, including South African audiences in 2004.

Phantom of the Opera could be read at several levels. It is a poignant archetypal love story of the fusing of the mind, body and soul of two romantics (Christine Daae and Vicomte Raoul) as well as a typical love triangle involving the deformed musical genius (The Phantom – Angel of Music), Christine Daae (the subject of both his love desire and artistic development, which he guides), and Raoul (The dashing, swashbuckling, chivalrous nobleman and later the lady he is besotted passionately to and deeply in love with). The musical could still be studied as the conquest of fear, of self-becoming and self-realization, of the triumph of the human artistic and creative spirit over existential disabilities.

Yet, as a very popular fable about the beauty and the beast, we also witness a lonely soul's search for redemption from the prison of moral depravity and spiritual corruption, in which his physical deformity is but a backdrop to a deeper disease of the soul. While he dwells in the catacombs beneath the Parisian Opera house, suffused by the dark waters of the sewage and the ethereal candlelight that barely illuminates his dark and dismal abode, the Phantom perpetually longs and yearns for freedom and release from his chamber of hell, from the torture of the Infernal Regions to the Elysian Fields of blessedness. It is this search for re-humanization and a wholesome connectedness with the sublime and the divine, the elevated and the noble, that sets him on the course of guiding and nurturing the prodigious talents of a chorus girl into a superstar diva of the stage.

His vision of Nirvana is thus structured as both a creative process and purgatorial sequences of escape, first by controlling the mind, thought and eventually body of his protégé, thereby gaining acceptance among humanity; and two by de-constructing the prevalent character and idiom of mundane and banal social relationship driven by polite society ("Insolent boy, this slave of fashion", "Ignorant fool, this brave young suitor, sharing in my triumph"!) in favour of the fusing and merging of creative spirit and passion in his hour of expected triumph.

At yet another level of meaning, *The Phantom of the Opera* explores the crisis of human culture and civilization, and in individuals, as specific units within a cultural milieu, by positing the vision that in every soul, and in the collective soul of a nation or a community, dwells all that is beautiful and ugly, enchanting and beastly. The struggle for the reconciliation of these opposite values, the tragic process it engenders, and the depths of despair, and sometimes of exoneration it can plunge a people, has been a primeval human instinct nourished over millennia, and an instinctual response to socio-cultural stimuli, which may be found in Joseph Conrad's *Heart of Darkness* (this idea does not in any way negate the racist – supremacist ideas in the book as many commentators have noted).

The musical celebrates the vision that out of the abundance of evil can emerge a sublime purpose in human life and human conduct because the search for social and cultural amelioration in the context of social and cultural obscurantism, and ultimately societal renewal, will come not by rejecting the ugly essences of reality but by transforming them. Christine, experiencing this dawn of a new spiritual consciousness, passionately kisses the Phantom not just because she wants to earn Raoul his freedom but because she has accepted his re-claimed humanity, and seen the beauty in him beneath the physical corruption, deformity and decay.

Through a series of beautifully written, haunting and well orchestrated songs, the theme of struggle, rivalry, redemption, reconciliation, growth in artistic consciousness and profound creative imagination unfolds with grace and matchless intensity and poignancy. From the Phantom – induced embarrassment of La Callota by causing the high proscenium canvas to fall on her, in her rehearsal of "Think of Me" to Christine Daae's choice as the singer – the Phantom's master strategy – and her beautiful, superlative and divine delivery of that song of remembrances of love lost-fleeting, intangible and eternally changing and transiting along unknown and unknowable paths; and from the imaginative reconstruction of her mental possession by the Phantom in "Angel of Music/The Journey" sequence that reaches its climax in the "Music of the Night" (an exultation by the Phantom about his conquest of Christine who would begin a new, unknown life which he incarnates), the musical gathers pace, picks up the action and advances its conflicts.

The Phantom's curse: "You will curse the day/you did not do what the Phantom/asked of you" that follows his loss of Christine to Raoul at their singing of the duet "All I ask of You" which presages his revenge action at the celebratory "Masquerade" dance drama exhibition (a sort of engagement night for Raoul and Christine) is followed by his confrontation with Raoul beside the tomb of Christine's father, a sword fight that perfectly sets the stage for "The Point of No Return". While a surface reading of "The Point of No Return" may suggest the Phantom's last desperate attempt to win back Christine and achieve a sexual union with her (the whole image of Don Juan and his carnal conquests is evoked here), its deeper implication is the phantom's despairing plea to Christine to see beneath his surface beastliness and witness the humanity that lies hidden.

Reluctantly, Christine betrays him again, and this unleashes a tragic sequence of events, the greatest being the crashing of the chandelier and the destruction of the opera house, and ends with her spiritual and physical union with the Phantom who, exhilarated and intoxicated with this acceptance, orders Christine and Raoul to "go now" and not reveal what they have seen at the murky, echoing catacombs. Yet to travel down this path of reconciliation the Phantom lamented:

Down once more to the Dungeons of my despair
Down we plunge to the Prison of my mind
Down that path into Darkness deep as hell

Hounded by everyone
Met with hatred everywhere
No kind words from anyone
No compassion anywhere

Why Christine,
Why

This becomes the bleeding chord in Christine's mass of conscience, her ultimate conviction about the attainment of a new state of knowledge about the Phantom's deep humanity.

The only additional comment about the musical is an account of the character of the all-knowing, yet unobtrusive dance instructor/choreographer, Madam Giry, the centre of consciousness that pervades the whole dramatic atmosphere with subtle, evocative power. She alone knows the riddle of the enigmatic Phantom, his sense of pain and solitude, his anguish and damnation. She alone, as Christine's guardian, knows equally her sense of loss, longing for creative attainment and highly imaginative and impressionistic mind. She connects the past to the present, understands the Phantom more than anyone else, has deep and moving sympathy towards him, and is ambivalent to Raoul at the beginning. Yet, she is the catalytic agent of reconciliation and redemption by first enlightening him about the sources of this "genius, musician, architect and composer" for him to appreciate the challenges that he faces and the obstacles he must surmount, and second, by leading him down the path of the catacombs, an eerie world in which, to survive, he must keep "his hand at the level of his eyes", wherein the Phantom is keeping Christine as a bait for the testing of his chivalry and depth of need.

Upon reflecting on the musical, *The Phantom of the Opera*, with specific reference to Nigeria, a number of things readily came to my mind. What hope have Nigerian audiences of ever watching such a musical on Nigerian soil? What are the prospects of popularizing this artistic tradition either through the importation of performers from overseas or its adaptation and domestication by local creative resources? Answers to these posers come in the negative because of the obvious incoherent state of our national culture. A cultural policy with the capacity of mobilizing the richness of indigenous cultural resources and engendering and enabling the environment for cultural progress is non-existent. Corporations that earn, often times, unjustified and unjustifiable profit, develop no structures, plans and strategies of giving back to society just a meager fraction of its stolen patrimony. They fund no cultural events, erect no cultural and artistic monuments and institutions, endow no cultural foundation and, in mentality, social psychology and spiritual disposition, they all seem to have, Philistine-like, turned their backs on the arts, and other creative forms of cultural expression.

Stifled by poor funding, and materially asphyxiated by the prevalent obscurantist cultural norms of the ruling elite, centres of artistic and cultural knowledge, mostly universities, schools and colleges of humanities (which include departments of music) are clearly exhausted, steeped as they are in a state of decadence. Musical compositions remain abandoned on dusty shelves, as creative spirits are manacled by the absence of proper theatres, opera houses and full orchestras either in the nation's capital or other provincial or regional locations. The tragedy of this situation is such that even if, given the raging fire of nationalism and decolonization, foreign musical materials that putatively purvey alien values, precepts and consciousness should not be promoted at home, who is presently, and strategically funding researches into indigenous verbal art forms and the musical resources of Nigeria's ethnic, national and cultural groups? Who has endowed scholars, artists and composers to unearth the nation's rich orature and various musical repertoires, traditional and contemporary? What, one may ask, is the present state of our operatic music, our dance drama, our total communal theatre?

Serious musical and theatrical activities are only sustained by men and women with an extraordinary stubborn will and uncommon devotion to their profession, in a few travelling theatres and musical ensembles, in a number of universities, and at the MUSON centre in Lagos. In large parts, the urge for cultural release is only attained among a few privileged elite who gather periodically at the Goethe Institute, the US and Germany Embassies, and at the French Cultural Centre for occasional evenings of songs, dance, classical musical sketches or Jazz performances.

Conclusion

Like the Phantom, Nigeria is in dire need of cultural redemption and re-humanization. Stupefied by the current reign of cultural unbelief and faithlessness, which reaches its high water mark in the obscurantist cant of a fickle-minded and unenlightened political and economic elite who have systematically led society to the dark dungeons of despair, moral miasma, ethical decay and anomie, atrophy and angst, and on the strength of that, to the brink of collective cultural immolation, the nation and its people have become as grotesque as the Phantom, riddled by physical deformity and spiritual waste. A cultural wasteland, Nigeria needs to begin an urgent process of cultural re-invention and transformation which has, like Christine and the Phantom, the capacity of reconciling the beast in us with the beauty that the land is pristinely endowed with.

At a more dangerous and alarming level, *The Phantom of the Opera* illuminates Nigeria's tragic historical and political process in the deliberate attempt, across the decades, but most particularly at this contemporary phase of historical evolution, of transfiguring a beautiful land with immense promise, potentials and possibilities, into a haunting, dark, and deformed beastly order. This journey towards Golgotha without the transubstantiating elixir of its biblical parallel only echoes an imminent apocalyptic void and eschatological fear, not only at the social, political and economic realms but at the very spiritual soul of the land. Increasingly, the national search of Elysium has led the people, not even to the purgatory boundaries of the Valley of Oblivion, but to the dank, putrefying and dark waste of the Infernal Regions.

The culture of impunity whereby national resources are pillaged and agglutinated without restraint by all manners of buccaneers and invidious influence-peddlers combines with a certain death of outrage to create a society permanently reeling under monumental moral embarrassment that is increasingly becoming ordinary happenstances, an accepted rhythm of an absurd existence. With lip service paid to transparency and accountability, moral probity and good governance, corporate responsibility and corporate citizenship, it is not surprising that the nation has lost its way, and like the Phantom, is so disfigured that genius has pertinently turned into madness. A redemptive process is again required in the conduct of the political and economic affairs of the state, with passion, commitment and courage, capable of leading society out of the path of national hallucination, disconnection and collective dissociation of sensibility to the purifying light of all that is beautiful, sublime, wholesome and noble.

Chapter

14

❦

LP AND MJ: THE TRIUMPH OF
IMMORTALITY

One died in his home town of Modena, after a fairly long and well advertised battle with pancreatic cancer, very much aware of the terminality of his condition and, awaiting stoically, proudly and triumphantly, for his transition into "immortality", having at least clocked three score and ten years. The other died of heart failure from preventive, drug-related, causes, biologically in the prime of life and in the midst of the exhilarating preparation for his sum up concert: "This is it". One was ebullient, exuberant, earthy, and extroverted, lived life to the zest and was constantly consumed by the passion of self-declaration and the intimations of mass adulation and applause.

The instant communicability of his massive frame, expressed in the "heroic brilliance" of his vocal range, assured for him an extraordinary universal presence that was matchless and peerless. The other was frail, withdrawn to the point of reclusion, shy, preferring the easy and innocent companionship of children and pet animals, only achieving a magical transformation on stage, whereupon he cast off the befogging cloak of insecurity in an electrifying burst of energy, guile, perfection and balance unsurpassed since the dawning of popular music as a technical and theatrical phenomenon.

One was a classical operatic tenor, who transformed the immortal arias of Donizetti and Verdi, Puccini and Wagner, Rossini and Leoncavallo, to mention but a few of the masters, into magical pieces of musical, artistic and cultural illumination. And in that process broke down the boundaries and limits of the human voice and transfigured an elite pastime into an accessible cross-over medium of eternal cultural expression, enacting in its wake a global cult followership with millions of devotees and acolytes. The other was a pop songwriter, singer and producer who arrested the imagination of millions with a soulful melody that can rise to the harsh croak of a metallic rocker, from "I Will Be There" to "Beat It," and from "ABC" to "Black or White"; who shattered racial-cultural antipathies with music that expressed an eternal universal tragic-comic condition; whose concerts, stage performances and music videos forever changed the face, nature, structure, character and essence of pop musical culture; and whose restricted appellation as the "King of Pop" was a studied deferment to Elvis, for unarguably he was indeed the King of Pop, Rock and Soul, the greatest pop icon of all time and the most influential ambassador of popular musical phenomenon.

What did Luciano Pavarotti, the Italian-born quintessential operatic tenor and lyric dramatist who changed the format and expanded the range, appeal and accessibility of operatic music and Michael Jackson, the African-American pop artist who redefined the boundary of popular music culture and foregrounded music video as an enchanting instrument for the communication of emotion, passion and feeling in ground breaking performances have in common? What could so forcefully, inexorably and intricately interconnect a classical artist whose breathtaking performance during "The Three Tenors" concert in Rome in 1990, particularly his rendition of Puccini's "Nessum Dorma" that held billions in the world spellbound, and a pop idol who shattered pop musical illusions with the "Thriller" album and attained unparalleled heights – universal encomiums and adoration – with the "Live in Bucharest: the Dangerous Tour", arguably the greatest pop musical concert extravaganza in recorded human history?

One word connects one to the other: genius. It is a word that carries with it an enormous spiritual burden, and is sometimes clothed with a tragic aura. A genius, like a tragic hero, is one who is set apart from the rest of mankind; who has the capacity to bridge the distance between illumination and consciousness; and who deploys and advertises his materiality with a force that is transcendental in quality. The search for immortality, which is a constant intuitive and instinctual desire of all mankind, is instantly possessed by the genius as a natural quantity that does not require constant labour. Yes, hard work, self-sacrifice, a narrow-minded, fanatical devotion to a cause or a calling and even luck are capable of transforming brilliance into manifest special gift, but the space a genius occupies is much wider in scope and range. It is a space defined by history and natural selection, a space that attests to the highest affirmation of human consciousness across millennial sweeps.

A genius is like an avatar, a mystical epigone that harbours the ideals of the universe at their highest point of exultation, and by so doing shatters the mechanical devices that separate realms of nature into unacceptable compartments. By crossing the boundary of preservation and perpetuation into the surreal region of immortality, a genius does that which no other man is capable of doing: he alters the rhythm of existence, supplants existing reality with its higher form and changes forever the spirit and soul of a generation. It is this transformative quality of the genius that sometimes wreaks a measure of psychic disorder in the individual, a sense of solitariness that cannot be compensated with the unfurling of mass adulation, even worship.

The path of the genius is a lonely course, a constant season of quietude in the sea of the tumultuous din he has unleashed. It is a complex journey of eternal balancing, between a ravaged individual identity and collective idolatry; between the gregarious necessities of natural living and the divinity he has been forced to claim; and between the insufferable scrutiny of his personal life and conduct and the effusive display of unfettered love by those who hold him to be infallible.

Those who have walked this lonely path are few – Edward de Vere, the 17th Earl of Oxford who wrote the immortal works of Shakespeare, and Descartes, Goethe and Wagner, Nietzsche and Marx, and of course Lenin, Einstein, Freud and Jung. They appear as enduring meteors, forged by the smithy of our collective unconscious, the essence of the inscrutable depths of human dawning. They carry the constant burden of historical clarification and elucidation, of identities and manners, of culture and science, of knowledge and epiphany.

The tragedy of being a genius is exaggerated in the conduct of those amongst them who are commonly held to have deviated from the common bounds and obligations of the rest of humanity. On the one hand, they are expected to exalt human passion and enrich human soul in a manner none can do. They are expected to constantly overreach themselves, spiritually drain their very psyche, in order to supply the cultural and other elixir that are beyond the imagination of ordinary folks. Yet they are held up to the same standards of behaviour like the rest of humanity, are subject to national and universal laws and moral codes and are restrained by the institutions created in the public domain – the media, law officers and the judicial system.

The force of this tragedy is demonstrated glaringly in the

life of Michael Jackson – complex, complicated but perfectly in harmony with the sensibility of being a genius. From President Obama who had to balance his tribute between the excess of his gifts and talents and the "tragedy of his personal life" to talking heads and pundits who point out the apparent divide between his musical consciousness and accomplishments and certain "troubling" facets of his material existence – the theme park called Neverland, the "abnormal" love for children, the child molestation charges, the surgeries, the dependence on prescription drugs, transformative personality, "weird" lifestyle, etc. – a picture emerges of a schizophrenic that in one breath can transport us from the dizzying pleasures and splendours of Elysium to the venality of the Infernal Regions. Yet, these commentators have not paused to ask why such a figure has the capacity to harbour such extremely contradictory traits and why in spite of that he gave mankind a quality and an essence it previously lacked, and why precisely, at his death, the earth literally froze, numbed into forced quietude, collectively mourning his passage without reservation, without rationalism, without scientific objectivity.

The crisis of human institutions, with particular regard to the genius, is that they are crafted by "ordinary" people to regulate the behaviour and conduct of "ordinary" people. Such institutions are not designed to accommodate the consciousness and sensibility of those who are "extra-ordinary"; who by virtue of special gifts are set apart from the rest of society and whose social martyrdom can only be compensated by the joy and happiness such gifts give to the rest of humanity. Geniuses have no place within the context of those institutions. A crippling universal moral and ethical ethos erected by a pertinently ordinary theocratic-political ruling groups hamper a genius from expressing his or her "reality" to the full. He could be hunted down, abused, handcuffed, jailed or even executed on the determinants of those institutions by policymakers and executors who in the privacy of their homes marvel at the extraordinary talent of the genius, the extraordinary happiness he generates which cannot be gotten elsewhere and the uplifting of the human spirit and soul, which only he can engender. Yet, these masters of public institutions, by denying the genius the ample social space he should and must inhabit, hold him to the same standard as they hold others, expect from him the same manner of conduct as he would expect from others and are perfectly at peace with themselves in applying on them the same rules and regulations others are subject to.

From beyond good and evil to the revaluation of values, the essence of the human journey must become the appreciation of the life of a genius as total harmony, as an indissoluble link and affinity between self-contained entities that find expression in various directions, and the impossibility of isolating those tendencies that are universally acclaimed as the work of a genius, an avatar, a master of consciousness from those that are held up to be low in moral, ethical or spiritual content, essence or quality.

A genius – warts and all – is a special, total package that must be understood in relation to his extraordinary abilities and gifts and must be constantly shielded from the vagaries and nuances of the mundane atmosphere and ordinariness which the rest of society inhabit. Special institutions are required to not only groom geniuses, but to nurse them into fruition. They ought to be judged solely on the terms set by such institutions, from the legal system, to criminal justice and from marriage to child bearing. Existing social institutions stifle the need for a genius to express himself in several directions.

Thus hampered, he retreats into his shell, inhabiting a shadowy, occult world of broken images and shattered mirrors, navigating a trenchant world of multiple identities and expectations and constantly wearing the cloak of schizophrenia – a balancing act between the propulsive desire of uninhibited self-declaration and even exaltation, and the reality over-determined by common sanction.

Geniuses are inherently over-disempowered in today's universe via a heavy laden dose of all manners of attenuating cultural, social and moral expectations that constrict value, deny it affirmation and render in-authentic its self-reinvention.

It is only when humanity attains this height of separating from its common mass, the few special ones in its midst, and ensuring the preservation, perpetuation and eventual immortality of their life, identity and essence that the tree of cultural liberty can be watered. And only through it can we become instantly appreciative of the fact that from cradle to grave the life of Michael Jackson, the genius, was perfectly charted and ordered in recognition of his apartness, from his father's early handling to his physical transformation, from his love of children and animals to his so-called "weird" lifestyle.

Conclusion: A Note on the Immortal State

Immortality is conventionally described as a transcendental phenomenon, a triumph over eschatological terror and an affirmation of ecclesiastical dreams. Immortality is also adjudged as the extension of the boundaries of humanity in a non-material context, a negation of the notion of "original sin" whereupon death visited mankind, and though this negation, an assured communion with the Godhead and other divine forces.

Yet, this notion of immortality is a revolt against material culture, for if anything, the immortal state is a terrestrial reality, a search for constancy, performance and enhancement by all values through the logic and process of their production, affirmation and self-re-invention. Man, the highest value in nature, searches for this attainment through preservative and perpetuative mechanisms and strategies, both in concrete, material images and symbolisms he erects and codifies, and via the means of cultural transcendence, whereupon he transfers material expectations in a reconstructed transcendental realm that is endowed with material properties and qualities, as a safeguard and an insurance against the uncertainties of earthly existence.

The first to attain the immortal stature are the geniuses of all generations, from science to philosophy, and from music to the arts, and in this specific context Luciano Pavarotti and Michael Jackson. TV programmes about "The Immortals" in sports and entertainment abound and many take them readily for granted, least suspecting that it perfectly justifies and affirms such terms as "Let's Immortalize Him"... "Let's build a monument to enshrine his name forever in our memory"... "Let's dedicate a school, name a street, a building, an airport, to ensure that his name never dies".

The Catholic doctrine is rich in this symbolism, for the Canonized Saints are immortalized first on earth before elsewhere, and their names are borne from generation to generation by the rest of us. By so doing, they defy death, and triumph over humanity, while the permanence of their memory, their ideas, their consciousness and life works are assured. While the rest of ordinary humanity struggle gallantly, and often-times vainly, to translate perpetuation into immortality the geniuses in our midst, like Pavarotti and Jackson, have already, instantaneously, attained a self-described and collectively sustained immortal state.

Man's search for the immortal path is to be seen in several cultures where the absence of a male child who will carry on and sustain the family lineage (immortality) is seen as a social, cultural and spiritual tragedy. Marriages are regularly broken and reconstituted in the quest for a male offspring, and if reports are right, in China, with the adoption of the one-child state policy, pregnancies are regularly terminated if the fetus is a female embryo. The climax of this quest, its apogee, its ultimate exultation is, first, through stem cell research that will yield life-mutants as bodily spare parts, and finally through cloning, a perfectly natural and rational path of attaining the immortal state.

Happily, neither Pavarotti nor Jackson suffered any

terrible accident that would have warranted sustaining their life and extraordinary performances with the products of stem cell research, and even Pavarotti's death – the result of the infanthood of the human enterprise, together with its medical, scientific and technological advertisements – is tragic as an expression of the limit of human nature, human capacity and human will. The only joy we will forever nurse is that whether he lived 10 or 20 years more, would have made no difference, his immortality having long been established and guaranteed.

Regarding the immortal state, I wrote as follows in **Autonomy of Values (Chapter Two: Cultural Reinventions: Belief, Faith and The Immortal Instinct...)**

> Beneath all philosophic constructions (regarding ethics and morality) lies the inescapable social and cultural fact of all times: the will to preserve, perpetuate and immortalize. A moral world order remains ordered only in the constancy of its affirmation. This is nothing short of self-regulated continuance of idea made fact. Things will only retain their collective quality in the process of renewal. This is self- perpetuation by other means. Man remains a political animal if he still has a family, community or state to grasp and hold; his very political quests, contests and endurance are the instinctual facts of his desire for immortality. The will to power, for example, explains this instinctual fact about man's search for immortality, for what is willed to become, as a consequence of overcoming, is not power in itself, but power to effectuate existential victory. It is not fame or wealth, but the capacity to triumph over existential odds ...
>
> ... If we re-examine the issue of the reproduction of species, especially with regard to self-perpetuation, (of which eugenics and cloning are part), we would not be startling mankind with an original cultural

insight. We will be merely asserting a fact of existence long denied. Anti-cloning legislation is a reaction against man's desire for immortality, and because it runs counter to human nature, is bound to be ineffectual ...

... It is clear that the immortal instinct, which includes any preservative and perpetuative assertion, is an autonomous value in man's estimation of self. As a principal law of nature and cultural survival, its attunement to human nature must be continually emphasized. The battle for man's dominance on the planet earth, against all other challenges, cannot be won by narrow-minded, self-limiting bio-ethical legislations that hamper the exercise of this will ... What ought to be championed is the cause of biological regulation of succeeding and even supplanting species, so as to establish an enduring nexus between the primeval instinct for immortality and the present day quest for self-perpetuation.

... without realizing it, Charles Krauthammer, in a *Time Magazine* essay, "Of Headless Mice... and Men", enters the record books as a master of illumination by bringing to public attention the potentially limitless possibility of bio-technology in fulfilling man's quest for immortality. His understanding that science has the capacity of creating "unconscious" life to aid the full and efficient functioning of "productive" life is one of the most potent cultural statements of our age. If we disregard his anti-cultural illusions regarding man's preservative instincts; his "excess of hysteria"; and his near absolute dependence on a constricting universal ethical order erected by a jealous ruling caste as organs of thought, what remains of his insights is a studied concession to the original design of man's existence – an innate quest for immortality founded on a deep-rooted cultural instinct.

Let us sample some of his thoughts:

> When prominent scientists are prepared to acquiesce in – or indeed encourage the deliberate creation of deformed and dying quasi-human life, you know we are facing a bio-ethical abyss. Human beings are ends, not means. There is no grosser corruption of bio-technology than creating a human mutant and disemboweling it at our pleasure for spare parts.

Response:

A human mutant is an inarticulate, un-affirming entity. Its consciousness of self is non-existent. Such a bio-technological creation can thus only assist in realizing the potentials of beings that are already incarnated with full awareness of self, and particularly that group of mankind whose exercise of will is not directed at self-affirmation but at the resolution of challenges that face the future existence of mankind. Let us take an example. If three scientists who are on the verge of discovering a vaccine against AIDS virus are to be involved in a road accident, and the condition of whose continued existence is dependent on multiple organs transfer that only bio-technologically created human mutants could readily provide, what will constitute the core moral and cultural question in relation to the future happiness of humanity? The obvious fact – not the truth – of the matter is that Krauthammer's standpoint is a sum product of the ethical prejudices of his cultural milieu, particularly the reverential treatment of the human body which is directly patterned after the image of "God", to the extent that a loss of one of God's own creation imposes a damaging ethical burden on the millions of beneficiaries whose collective empowerment is dependent on that loss. Krauthammer's standpoint is thus neither scientific nor cultural in its material sense, but rather a romantic allegiance to culture-in-transcendence – which in its own expansive though problematic context is a form of legitimation of man's immortal instinct.

i.   "The prospect of headless human clones should put the whole debate about "normal" cloning in a new light. Normal cloning is less a treatment for infertility than a treatment for vanity. It is a way to produce an exact genetic replica of yourself that will walk the earth years after you "are gone".

Response:

I do not know precisely when and why man's quest for self-succession has become an idle, vain pastime. Man has always demanded of himself the cultural competence to outlive his determinate realm. Religion speaks volumes about this. In material life, his exploration of this principle has created for human civilization immortal icons from where references are always drawn. The author of the works of Shakespeare is surely not materially aware of his immortality, yet, he remains an immortal icon. So are Plato, Aristotle, Marx, Nietzsche and Freud. Now, for man the possibility is opening up for the translation of his capacity for immortality from a future prospect (at which state he is materially unconscious of that fact) to a material condition in which he can affirm that possibility in his lifetime, and he is called vain. Here, as before, the scientific-cultural issue in cloning is not and should not be tailored to suit the productive and replicative nuances of just any human stock or gene pool, but must be directed at the careful selection, replication or sustenance (via bio-technological mutation of "still" life) of advanced human species. Here, again, as before, infertility or humanitarian gestures should play no part nor achieve any relevance in this cultural process.

ii.   "The headless clone solves the facsimile problem. It is a gateway to the ultimate vanity: immortality. If you create a real clone, you cannot transfer your consciousness into it to truly live on. But if you create a headless clone of just your body, you have created a ready source of replacement parts to keep you – your consciousness – going indefinitely".

Response:

Man created the original immortal instinct by transferring his consciousness of transcendence from an unrealizable material realm to an extra-terrestrial plane of divinity. Since that creation, his consciousness has been focused in one direction – a self-preservative quest that has taken him to religion, mysticism, occultism, and, today, in the new age cultic groups. This has been his pristine cultural wish – to live forever, in eternity, and to sustain his awareness of self in life-after. Now, at last, he has within his grasp, a certain reversal of his immortal instinct: he can actually re-translate his wish from a transcendental plane to a material one. Cloning is the first step; the second is the replication of unconscious life from where conscious existence could be extended indefinitely. Man is thus on the verge of a major scientific-cultural breakthrough which will make nonsense of his puny efforts in dieting, healthy living, physical fitness and obsession with vitamins and anti-ageing mendicants. And Charles Krauthammer calls this ultimate vanity:

"Who in fact among us will really desire death (a source of immortality-in-transcendence) if indeed he could live in eternity on earth in full health, and in full possession of his consciousness and other capabilities? If this point must be re-stressed, we will come to the inevitable conclusion that the passion for immortality will be fed with more than a dose of narcissism. It needs a stronger narcotic – the narcotic of cultural preservation, and with that the endurance of individual and collective human species. And because this passion is in favour of natural laws and logic, it must always aflame man's consciousness in whatever direction that it finds space, in spite of all legislations to the contrary.

iii. "Congress should ban human cloning now totally. And regarding one particular form, it should be draconian:

the deliberate creation of headless humans must be made a crime, indeed a capital crime. If we flinch in the face of this high tech barbarity, we'll deserve to live in the hell it heralds"*.
(*All quotations from Time Magazine, January 19, 1998, p.56).

Response:

I wonder who "we" are. Surely it doesn't include scientific researchers, bio-technological experts, medical personnel, beneficiaries of the cloning process etc., all who must be living in the twilight zone of the prevailing moral orthodoxy, all who must be indeed mad, and all whose sense and idea of culture and self-preservation must be indeed weird and out of this world. Krauthammer addresses no real scientific or cultural issue here. His sense of loss is nothing but the pathetic outpouring of a man unaware of the real essence of values, all values, particularly the value that nature has jealously incarnated in its own primary image; the value of man as a cultural product, and the value of culture as man's permanent, irreversible search for self-preservation, and ultimately, for immortality.

I first wrote this in 1998. I still stand by it today.

AFTERWORD

Nigeria is still in search of a theme. The sense of collective national dissociation of sensibility is explained, in part, by the absence of a coherent national ideological and philosophical platform that propels belief and faith. National values are thus, not the systematization of the pool of values derived from the nation's federating ethnic, cultural, linguistic, religious and class coalitions but the interplay of semi-autonomously existing value types playing out on the national stage.

With defective key governance instruments, over-burdened institutions and near incoherent social processes, the democratic transition, oftentimes, bears an embarrassing aura. Yet, even with the spectre of national incompleteness, and the scars of a civil bloodbath, multiple military political eruptions and a near pathological predilection of a bunch of its ruling elite towards social parasitism as the only substance of their covenant with the people, the nation stubbornly clings on hopes.

That hopeful faith about a yearned for elixir for the amelioration of social and cultural maladies is not the self-arrested triumph of illusion over reality, mirage over existence, but a testament to the elemental force of humanity, in its tragic majesty and inscrutable logic. It is the idea that the people and their land will endure, because they willed it so. It is the inexplicable testimony of man's inherent indestructibility in the face of weighty challenges. It is also a manifestation of the philosophical truth that the human condition has an infinite capacity for tolerance and self-exoneration in opposition to collective immolation, the purificatory rite of which is the commitment of the many, through the social act of trans-substantiation, to cleanse a land polluted by a few, by the way of collective suffering.

Without a doubt, a National Positive Force is awakening, and re-arming itself with the tools of intellect, knowledge and hard work. Whether as ideas men and women, as institution builders, as guardians of the sacred human gift of freedom and liberty, or as dedicated artisans, entrepreneurs and farmers, a national ferment is in the making, mastering its course, awaiting its season, measuring its dawning ... It is this force that will guide the nation along the path of self-discovery. It is this force that will ensure the triumph of the national democratic enterprise through the liberation of the human spirit and the un-caging of human consciousness. It is this force that will make real and permanent the realization of the Nigerian possibility in a universe of quantum leaps and unceasing transformation.

APPENDIX

SIX ESSAYS ON ARMED WORDS

1. Armed Words
2. Our National Zombie Ethic
3. Combating the Zombie Mentality
4. How Many Are We Really in Nigeria? 1
5. How Many Are We Really in Nigeria? 2
6. The Illogic of Revenue Allocation

These essays were published in the 7AM NEWS EXTRA newspapers between March and April, 2010. They were part of my weekly back page column, which ran from March to September, 2010, when I took up appointment as the Director-General of the Dr Abubakar Bukola Saraki presidential campaign organization. I had already put out in a booklet form a reworked version of six other essays from the column titled "Rotation of Power and Igbo Possibility: Toward the 2015 Presidency Project." I hope to publish, before long, the entire essays that made up the column in a single collection.

1. *Armed Words*

When my good friend Anselm Okolo invited me to chair the Editorial Board of 7AM NEWS EXTRA and contribute a weekly back page column I experienced an instant rush of adrenalin on the prospect of having a platform to express views which I hold so dearly. However, my sheer, almost unbridled excitement quickly gave way to an acute moment of introspection. What, again, is yet to be written and said about a nation that has lost its way and whose elite behave like members of the cargo cult so hauntingly described by Ayi Kwei Armah in *Fragments*? What further word can pierce the scaffold of unreason that has manacled the soul of a generation, inspiring nothing but a sense of collective national idiocy? After all, over a century and half ago, a certain Karl Marx had declared that philosophers have described the world in several ways, the only problem being how to change it.

Yet, I do admit that the mass media have played a crucial role in periods of national distress and uncertainty. Three great moments stand out in this regard: the struggle to validate the result of June 12, 1993 Presidential election which the late Chief M.K.O. Abiola won and to end the season of military despotism; the struggle against the pseudo neo-messianic propensity of former President Olusegun Obasanjo which reached its hallucinatory degree in the third term agenda; and the current national debate over the place and purpose of presidential power in the nation's evolving constitutional governance.

With this inspiring thought in mind, I reached the conclusion that my friend's faith in the viability of yet another newspaper as a mode of social intervention is not misplaced, and neither is it a waste of time and space in having a column which will join the ranks of the vibrant ones already in the public domain.

In penning this inaugural essay – from which will be gleaned the style and substance of the pieces that will address specific issues – I sought to define my ideas in the words, thoughts and minds of individuals whose intellect has continued to inspire me. For example, in *Writers in Politics*, Ngugi wa Thiong'O asserts that whether he is aware of it or not, a writer's works –

> ... reflects one or more aspects of the intense economic, political, cultural, and ideological struggles in a society. What he can choose is one or the other side in the battlefield: the side of the people, or the side of those social forces and classes that try to keep the people down. What he or she cannot do is to remain neutral. Every writer is a writer in politics. The only question is what and whose politics ...

Ngugi went on to give us the symbolism of Armed Words, the verbal and written craft of liberation – both of consciousness, and in social practice – in the image of Matigari who effortlessly interprets the logic of freedom as the paradigm of armed resistance through vocal militancy.

Ngugi's thought is not far from that of Franz Fanon who reminded us that "every generation must, out of relative obscurity, discover its mission, fulfil it or betray it," and who also warned that –

> ... the future will have no pity for those (especially members of the intellectual, cultural and artistic elite) who, possessing the exceptional ability to speak words of truth to the oppressors, have instead taken refuge in an attitude of passivity, mute indifference, and sometimes, of cold complicity...

Two other exponents of Armed Words are recalled here. We call to mind the courage of the African-American liberationist, Fredrick Douglas, who stated that –

> ...if there is no struggle, there is no progress. Those who profess to favour freedom, and yet depreciate agitation, are men who want crops without ploughing up the ground. They want rain without thunder and lightning. They want the ocean without the awful roar of its many waters...

We recall also the evocative narrative of Eduard Galeano whose matchless historical and mytho-poeic sequence of remembrances in *Memories of Fire and Open Veins of Latin*

America have a lot to instruct us in this regard. In "Defense of the Word" in *Open Veins* he declares that –

> ... Our own fate as ... a writer is linked to the need for profound social transformations. To narrate is to give oneself: It seems obvious that literature, as an effort to communicate fully, will continue to be blocked ... so long as misery and illiteracy exist, and so long as the possessors of power continue to carry on with impunity their policy of collective imbecilization ... through the mass media. Our effectiveness depends on our capacity to be audacious and astute, clear and appealing. I would hope that we can create a language more fearless and more beautiful than that used by conformist writers to greet the twilight ... A literature is taking shape and acquiring strength, a literature that does not propose to bury our dead, but to immortalize them; that refuses to stir the ashes but rather attempts to light the fire ... Perhaps it may help to preserve for the generations to come "the true name of all things ...

Who are the targets of media criticism in Nigeria? Historically speaking, successive regimes–corrupt, inept, despotic or downright stupid–together with their infirm, dysfunctional and mediocre bureaucracies and retinue of collaborators and panegyric singers have been at the receiving end of caustic media commentary, including highly imaginative cartoons. My brand of Armed Words will, of course, maintain and reinforce this tradition. But this is half the picture. Marx may have averred that the ideas of the ruling classes are the ruling ideas in every historical epoch, meaning that the classes that control material production invariably control mental and intellectual production mostly expressed in symbolic and imagistic terms and patterns. Yet, no amount of social and economic alienation can so attenuate the humanity, creative vitality and critical life force of a people as is witnessed in Nigeria, rendering the mass mentally pauperized, and their civil society platforms   perpetually mouthing incoherent cant and vacuous slogans. Armed Words will thus be targeted at the people, at their key institutions and platforms, with the hope that they can still reach down to the depths of their collective soul and begin their process of re-humanization.

In the coming weeks and months, I intend to use the resources of wit, satire, irony, scathing social criticism, lampoon, caricature and a refined brand of intellectual militancy to nudge public affairs discourse along the direction of engagement, intervention and critical action. To achieve this, I prepared for myself and for the consideration of the wider public a modest manifesto which is presented below.

I hold firm to the belief that an "individualized" thesis of social practice, which is rooted in iconoclastic ideas must ultimately be affirmed by the will of the collective: that is to say, those endeavours, which are primarily connected to the consciousness of an individual must depend on mass impulses and sanction for their coherent legitimation. Again, we need not draw a line between *ideas as the effect of social practice or social practice as, primarily, the only cause of creative ideas*. Intuitively, even without the recourse to the laws of dialectics, it is instantly apprehensible that while the foundation of any coherent social order must depend on the interlocking of ideas that define the scientific-technological, information and cultural space, with material images and values, which are concretely and constantly enhanced and sustained to ensure the survival of the social system, it is cognitively impossible to separate the two, codify them, compartmentalize them.

The crisis of the Nigerian State is to be seen in the sheer dissonance between the "intellectual content of the state" and the strategies deployed to effectuate social practice. This heightened level of dissociation has created a distance between the "ideas in the margin" on which must depend the survival of the state together with the health, welfare and happiness of its people, and the incoherent, often times, anarchic pursuit of a state of National Elysium by those who lead. Inexplicably, the outward manifestations of this disconnection – vacuous social materialism, indolence, mediocrity, dysfunctional state institutions, corruption, sleaze and graft – are passed off as indeed the cause of the nation's arrested social development. Very few opinions moulders and intellectuals haunted, as they are, by the crippling effects of poverty and mass destitution in the midst of the pompous display of buccaneered wealth, see the anti-cultural, anti-intellectual hallucinations of a spiritually empty and morally sterile ruling class as the main culprit.

The challenge before us is to re-establish this broken dialogue and connect the national navel to its hidden umbilicus through a pitiless and merciless assault on the reign of unreason that defines the public discourse space. By the unleashing of intellectual "war" on the spate of maddening falsehoods that characterize illusory assumptions on the idea of "Presidentialism", "Federal Character", "Power Shift", "Resource Control," "Fiscal Federalism" and "National Restructuring", to mention a few of the questions which appear settled in the minds of the intellectually lazy and indolent in our midst, we can begin the rite of national cleansing, a purgatorial sequence of ideas generation, dissemination and popularization that must, inexorably, render in-authentic and illegitimate all prevalent orthodoxies.

When the intellectual and ideas space is liberated and secured in the mainstream media, internet traffic and in public fora (seminars, workshops, and conferences etc. the space for social action speedily opens up, expands and becomes increasingly absorbent. A vanguard must thus be erected that will envelope in its fold the nation's finest minds in science and technology, industry and commerce, mass media, civil society, labour, political activism, the intelligentsia and among the ranks of conscious youths, to unfurl the banner of national awakening through mass mobilization, cell-building and strategic organization across all sectors and spheres.

It is thus quite possible that with inflexible will, iron determination, self-sacrifice, stoic resistance to threats and intimidation, and clarity of vision and focus, we can begin to re-build the land, and lay the solid foundation for the enthronement of a truly egalitarian, populist and genuinely democratic social order in Nigeria.

I can already hear the voices of the cynics in the land leering, *haba,* not again, another idealist in our midst? What the hell does he think he will achieve! Maybe, maybe not, only time will tell.

I have re-read Aesop's Fables of late and feel truly amazed at the similarity between these fabulous tales with contemporary Nigerian social, cultural and political condition. I will endeavour to end each weekly piece with one of his fables.

2. *Our National Zombie Ethic*

The late Afro-Jazz genius, Fela Anikulapo-Kuti's "Zombie" which he released in the early 1970s created so much musical, social and political sensation that was, arguably, unparalleled in the history of Nigerian music culture. It consolidated his position as Africa's pre-eminent musical artist, built a cult-like followership around his enigmatic personality, aroused social consciousness to an unprecedented degree, but most instructively directed the ire of the ruling military establishment against his counter-culture platform. The destruction of Kalakuta Republic was achieved, and the syndrome of the Unknown Soldier came to symbolize the authoritarian state apparatus.

A close reading of the lyrics of "Zombie" suggests that Kuti's scathing satire was directed at the military establishment and its apish mindset, an unbecoming social trait that Leo Tolstoy, the towering 19th century Russian novelist, equally lamented about, for those familiar with his novel, *Resurrection.* Happily enough, the military service of today is light years away from the coup-plotting, conspiracy-ridden armed forces of the 1970s, 1980s and the mid-1990s given its intellectual depth and confidence, the academic pedigree of its command staff, and the broad, far-reaching transformation of the security sector that has implanted on its key personnel the necessity of subjecting such forces to democratic and constitutional control.

The *Webster Comprehensive Dictionary* (Encyclopedia edition) defines a zombie as "the supernatural power by which a dead body is believed to be reanimated; specifically, a corpse reactivated by sorcery, but still dead." In West Indian mythic culture and occultist tradition such a reanimated corpse lacks a mind and will of its own, is dispossessed of social consciousness and power of critical reflection, and exists to do the bidding of its owner (menial work, hard-breaking farm labour, and even murder), without question, without protestation. From its earlier usage to characterize the behaviour of the nation's armed forces, the zombie phenomenon steadily crept into the Nigerian public service establishment where it still resides, and has today seeped into virtually all aspects of the national life within the social publics that define the nation.

As a director in one of the numerous federal government agencies that clutter the land, I was amazed by the level of the uncritical acceptance of all manners of official oddities and absurdities by members of staff who have been reduced to the status of zombie by the system. The willingness to carry out plainly stupid directives without question, to blindly implement policies one does not believe in without reservation or murmur, and to repeat exercises year in, year out, that are futile, without comment, was truly amazing. The battle I had in my hand was to constantly create a healthy balance between accepting the dictates of an apish, zombie public service mentality and my consciousness as a critical intellectual who must repose the privilege, if not, the right to say no to evil and other untoward social practices.

I will give but one example. For three years the agency I worked for, and which was set up to execute very vital social

mandates was never released a kobo allocation for its capital
projects. And this is how it works. The call circular for capital
projects, overhead expenses and personnel cost will be issued
around July or August. Innumerable meetings will be held
to prepare the budget which will be eventually defended at
the ministerial level, and subsequently at the National
Assembly before the relevant committees.

The same exercise could be repeated over four times,
sometimes followed by an oversight visit by the NASS
Committees. The agency goes back and waits with bated
breath for the capital vote to be appropriated. When the
budget is finally signed into law by the President, the agency
will discover that funds have been appropriated for personnel
cost and overhead expenses. It does not ask a question about
its capital budget allocation. Come next July-August, the
exercise begins afresh and at the end it still draws zero
capital allocation. Again, no question is tolerated.

Indeed, in my last three years at this particular agency,
zero capital allocation was drawn. Amazing, you will say.
But it happens all the time in several other agencies and
extra-ministerial departments, with their respective heads
and senior staff complacently accepting this absurd
situation, carrying on as if it is normal, and warning staff
to refrain from comments and utterances that may portray
them as insubordinate, recalcitrant and disloyal to the
system, were they to contemplate questioning this sickening
stupidity. I ended up drawing salary for three years for doing
virtually no work, except maybe executing micro-sized
programmes funded by international development partners.

Pray, tell me, if this is not *zombism*, what the hell is it?

The zombie mentality appears, operates and dominates the
social landscape in virtually all we do as a people, in the
casual acceptance and rationalization of official impunities,
intimidation, inefficiency and mis-governance. We see this
in educated men and women queuing for upwards of 72

hours at filling stations (even on Sallah and Xmas days), munching corn on cob, eating banana and chewing kola, cracking forced jokes, suffering, smiling, apparently without a care in the world. Guess what? After, maybe 72 hours of this debasing, dehumanizing and imbecilizing chore the man finally gets fuel, he quickly calls (or pings) his wife with an air of triumph, screaming on her eardrums, "Hi, honey; guess what? I have just got fuel. Tell them to run the bath for me. I will soon be home". The above scenario does not require elaborate commentary.

Pray, tell me, if this is not zombism in operation, what the hell is it?

We see this also in the standard behaviour of the Nigerian elite and petty elite when confronted with shocking news in the dailies or an inexplicable increase in the price of staple food. A man's attention is drawn to a headline about how some ministers, directors, or NASS members have frittered away N40bn of public fund and he is asking his friend about the increase in the price of *kpomo*. Tell him that a few highly placed individuals have walloped over $4bn meant for a critical development project, and he is worried about the price of eba. And if his house help returns empty handed, having gone to buy bread, with the story that the price has changed, he rails at her, wondering why she is so stupid as to not buy the one made with cassava.

Pray, again, tell me, if this is not zombism, what the hell is it?

No wonder that the late Prof. Sam Aluko once posited that the primitive economy such as ours can never collapse given the inexhaustible elasticity of human patience in this shore. If a man cannot afford *Semovita* for his family, he goes for pounded yam. If pounded yam is out of reach, he requests for *Akpu, Amala* or *Tuwo*. If he cannot afford any of this, he settles for *Alibo* or *Rogo*. The zombie mentality has drained Nigerians of their humanity, sapped their will to resist, foisted on all of us a culture of complacency and uncritical acceptance of official criminal conduct, pauperized our thought and famished our social consciousness.

Aesop's Fable
The Dove and the Crow
A dove locked up in a cage, was congratulating herself on how many children she had hatched, when a crow came by and said, "Stop boasting my friend! The more young ones you have, the more slaves there will be for you to groan over".
(What are we, in Nigeria today, but slaves in a cage, who pretend we are happy with our sordid condition?)

3.   *Combating the Zombie Mentality*
In our "Our National Zombie Ethic" I drew my readers' attention to a burgeoning national zombie mentality that has, like a raging malady, taken possession of the soul of the nation, and in the words of the poet, Oswald Mtshali, "ravaging it beyond despair". I located this phenomenon in the military establishment tradition of the 1970s, 1980s and 1990s and showed how it has spread like a cancer cell, which has "licked in to all corners" of the land. I gave a number of examples of this atavistic national norm which has drained our people of the capacity of free will, critical reflection and robust social consciousness.

The zombie story continues. Intellectually, I was fully conscious of the place of the zombie mind-set as perhaps the most fundamental drawback in changing our society for the better; in confronting the multiplicities of evil in the social system; and of saying no to the agents of obscurantism, tyranny and despotism who will never allow genuine democracy, constitutional governance, probity, human rights and equal access to opportunities to dictate the direction of the state. No doubt most of us see this in the indolence, mediocrity, non-performance, sheer mental laziness and inefficiency that power our public service, and indeed all our public institutions. The tragedy, of course, is not the impact of these negative traits, but our collective, Zombie-like readiness to accept them as normal, given, immutable, infinite ...

Yet, in terms of social experience, I was taught a lesson about the free, sovereign reign of this malady by a friend who asked that I take a ride with him around Abuja. He warned me that the spectacle I was about to witness will be like none other I had ever experienced. Curious, I asked him what social experiment he was about to conduct. His answer was a very simple one. He opined that Nigerians have been so imbecilized in the medical conception of the term that their reaction to any unpredictable behaviour is not a product of deep thought or critical consideration of the rational import of such behaviour. It is painfully, he said, a reaction that is ostensibly sheepish and conformist.

We drove beyond the city gate, along the airport with a heavy traffic behind us. Ahead of us stretched the broad highway, undisturbed by any obstruction-police barrier, suspicious clutter of vehicles or human beings. Nothing. He accelerated fast beyond Milipat Plaza, braked sharply and swung his vehicle to the left into the divide between the two highways. He then asked me to look back and witness the spectacle he had earlier spoken about. Every single vehicle behind us screeched to a halt, some turning off the road, and many looking for small road arteries they will dash into. Not one vehicle came near where we were. None made any attempt to move on. The road became frozen with sudden immobility. A few minutes later he drove out to the same road and we proceeded. Again, life came back to the road, engines were started and revved and the traffic surged on again. He repeated the same, you will say, risky experiment ten times all over the city with the same predictable result.

"You see", he leered at me with a grin, "we all have been reduced to mindless Zombies, thoughtless individuals who question nothing, evaluate nothing, but merely behave in a mass, well-conditioned pattern, incapable of taking our destiny in our hands, and unable to examine one another's behaviour critically to determine what is abnormal, unnecessary, illogical" . I could do nothing but marvel, because it is in the mass acceptance of the illogical, and the un-reflective and instinctual accommodation of social oddities that is deeply located the engine of a national Zombie culture.

Has anybody ever paused to observe the total disconnect between the people who engage in rallies, protest marches and peaceful demonstrations organized by the labour movement and her civil society allies to address issues that concern just about everybody? Whether such marches are organized to address the scarcity of petroleum products, the impending hare-brained attempt to deregulate the downstream petroleum sector or to canvas for electoral reform does not really matter. The marchers or protestors appear as a rag-army made up of quixotic individuals who appear completely isolated from the rest of the populace.

It is always troubling to observe such pathetic spectacles; of road users impatiently hooting their horns to get such nuisance out of the way, alarmed that their very banal appointment–may be a delicious dish of *Nkwobi* or Isi *Ewu* at their favourite restaurant is about to be ruined by people who cannot mind their business. On the curbs, door–ways and shop entrances will be massed curious onlookers, bemused that some people will be foolish enough to be marching in the sun, sweat pouring out of their faces, and probably harassed from pillar post by well-helmeted police men, some on horses' backs, with whip in their hand. Were the police to chase down the marchers, all around will be hooting and mocking laughter of the curious on-lookers, with not a few declaring to their neighbours, "serves the bastards right, why can't they mind their business. Trouble makers, they are getting what they deserve".

I know this from experience during my days as an EMU

and NADECO activist, giving our all against the military dictatorship of the late Gen. Sani Abacha. Not only did the mass of the people not participate in our protest marches and door to door distribution of leaflets, they warned us not to bring our trouble down to their doorsteps. At a certain point in time, the EMU chancery in Enugu became a ghost house, with only Dr Arthur Nwankwo, the EMU Chancellor, myself and a few die-hards to be seen in his residence which serves as the chancery, day in, and day out. We were totally isolated, cut-off, carrying on as best we could, not for personal gain, but for the overall interest of the national collective.

Maybe, the mobilizational tactics, the political education programme and the strategies of raising public consciousness of the March organizers are defective and not far-reaching enough. Maybe. Yet, I have a sneaky feeling that the problem is far deeper than this. In a social environment in which thought has been famished and critical reflection pauperized; in which people are but a shadow of themselves, over-burdened by the brutal struggle of daily material survival, what the hell can they do, you will ask? Many have given up hope on any meaningful interactive endeavour, atomized in regular conduct and contacts with their fellow human beings, and psychologically lobotomized to the point of nothingness. We, as creatures of a modern society that yields nothing to the individual, not through hard work, creative endeavour and talent, but through sly, cunning, greed, graft and sleaze, have given up hope of connecting with and to ourselves, and now lack the capacity of identifying with others to confront the great challenges of our time.

Maybe, one way out of this zombie mindset is to start building resistance from bottom up. While large civil society platforms are attractive because of their potential mass followership, and thus, the potential to do great rescue work, they are hampered by the limit set by deficient finance, and organizational and strategic incapacity. The people can begin to re-discover their humanity and cast out the cloak of zombism by organizing at the neighbourhood level. By creating cell-like structures in all neighbourhood centres across all the cities and towns in the nation, and in all communities and wards, they can begin to demand and get those things the larger groups can never achieve in the short run. They can print leaflets and share their concerns among themselves. And rather than use coal pressing iron to straighten out the wrinkles in their clothes or put on paraffin lamps, and for those who can afford it, their cranky, noisy generators, they should move in a disciplined fashion to the neighbourhood PHCN office and demand for light. Same for water, potholes on the roads, refuse disposals, etc. Maybe, if we begin at this level, we can exercise the ghost of zombism planted in our collective soul by an uncaring, life-reducing system.

Aesop's Fable

The Horse and the Groom

A dishonest groom used to steal and sell a horse's oats and grain on a regular basis. He would, however, spend hours busily grooming and rubbing him down to make him appear in good condition. Naturally the horse resented this treatment and said, "If you really want me to look well, groom me less, and feed me more."

(Nigerian leaders should not deceive the people with empty, decorative words. They should provide for their welfare and not steal their resources.)

4. How Many Are We Really in Nigeria? [1]

Let me make my position clear from the onset. I am not in any way disputing the official population figures put out by the National Population Commission which has pegged the population of Nigerians dwelling in Nigeria at 150 million. If you add the population of Nigerians living in the Diaspora, you may up the official estimate by at least 200 million. My grouse is not with this kind of estimate. It has entered the record books and is being, presumably, used for all manners of statistical evaluation of our national needs, and the strategic policy planners deploy to make life a little less harsh for Nigerians.

I will also hasten to make yet another point right away. I know that the official population estimate is a demographic fraud. Nobody really knows how many we are, not the President, State Governors, Federal and State Legislators and Chairpersons of the 774 Local Government Areas. I was a member of a government census monitoring team in 2006 during the last census exercise covering the South-South. Going by what we observed, the people we interviewed and my periodic excursion to Aba, Abia State from Port-Harcourt, it would be foolhardy for anybody to imagine that over 60% of Nigerians were really counted during that exercise. The 2006 census was an aberrant demographic fiction, plainly negotiated to sustain a pre-existing demographic fallacy.

The three planks of negotiation, compromise and demographic fiction have, in any event, always defined Nigeria's census exercises since 1963. Interestingly, the 1991 census, the basis on which the demographic variables of the 2006 exercise were arrived at, including but not limited to inter-censual growth rate, had the South-West population growing by only 1m from 1963 to 1991; had a number of local government areas actually recording significantly reduced population from the 1963 levels, and achieved a statistical dead hit with regard to the growth of the South-East between 1963-1991.

Interestingly, the title of this piece has very little to do with the viability of the current figures being bandied around as the population of Nigeria. It interrogates a different question altogether. If the population of Nigeria is indeed 150 million, does it then mean that there are real, existing, well-functioning human entities that make up that population; that is, beings who have all the noted characteristics of humans the world over; beings who think, talk, behave like and are generally endowed with qualities that define the human race?

As absurd as this question may appear, one key issue that is in operation here is not the quantity or number of beings that walk the land but the humanity of those beings. This is to stress that while there may indeed be 150 million beings who walk erect like human beings; who have all the external features of human beings; and who dwell in houses, work in offices and operate businesses that human beings are known to operate, are all these beings human in the strict sense of the term? Is it possible to posit that, based on observable conduct, general altitude and behaviour, there indeed may not be more than a few million humans out of the 150 million beings that the NPC says we are?

This may appear to be a shocking picture to paint, and being a humanist with deep consciousness and a sense of loyalty to all that is human, it's a question that I have agonized over for a long time. How many people are aware that a sense of social reclusion is steadily creeping into the Social System; that is, those who have voluntarily withdrawn from society, and only establish minimal contact with the rest simply because they can no longer stand the stupidity all around them? From the moment they step out of their houses to the time they come back home, their senses are assailed, violated and dehumanized by the beastliness, idiocy and organized lunacy that are vomited out in all social directions. Their only comfort zone is their house, and possibly their study, for those who still read, listen to good music and watch well-made movies. Such people's sense of isolation is as total as the outrage they experience in their daily contact with people, in the inexplicable, dysfunctional, chaotic, undisciplined and animalistic mindset of their contemporaries.

 I always engage my friend who indeed nudged my consciousness towards the need to separate the humans from the other erect beings that haunt the nation in spirited argument over his extremist mindset. He refused to be intimidated by my harsh, critical words to the effect that human beings cannot be perfect; that human flaws are natural; and that social idiocy and imbecility are integral parts of human existence. He was unyielding and unflinching in his thesis that millions of Nigerians have already crossed the threshold of reason, abandoned the human realm and are persistently dwelling in the nadir region of unbecoming and unbelief. For him this ethereal occult zone of irrationality has generated a whole system of attitude and conduct that cannot be classified as remotely human.

To prove his point on one score alone, he asked that I drive with him around town. He will only use the behaviour of road users, among thousands of other examples he can call up, to prove his point. Reluctantly, I switched off my video player at the beginning of the Triumphant March in Verdi's *Aida,* entered his car and off we went. Behind us was this taxi driver who was hooting his horn incessantly and apparently for no reason. After 5 minutes of our car being assailed by this beastly noise, my friend pulled over and signaled to the taxi-driver to stop. He beckoned to him and asked why he was hooting his horn. The taxi-driver looked at him uncomprehendingly, muttered something under his breath and slinked off. "You see," my friend grinned at me, "this fellow has long ceased to be a human being, and there is nothing you can do about his condition."

At the overhead bridge linking Wuse Market and Wuse II, one van apparently going to Wuse Market or Wuse Zone 6, stopped at the traffic light but blocked the exit to the Abacha expressway leading to Mabushi, etc. This exit should always be constantly free of traffic obstruction but the van driver just sat there without a care in the world. Behind him stretched a queue of vehicles, a kilometer long, horns hooting, all waiting to enter the exit to their various destinations. My friend stopped his car, which was right behind the van, walked up to the driver, and asked him pointedly, "are you also among the 150 million Nigerians?"

The van driver grinned sheepishly, unaware of the havoc he had unleashed behind him. My friend got back into the car, turned to me and said. "I told you so. Tick that one off. He cannot be among the 150 million people in the country."

A few other experiences on the road reluctantly convinced me that my friend may indeed have a point. Traffic lights are violated at will, at random, apparently without a care. A car taking the next left turn will rather be on the farthest right lane and you dare not stop him from cutting in front of you. Madness, lunatic behaviour, and inexplicable idiocy define road usage. Indeed, if you tick off all the beings involved in this, you may regrettably discover that we may never know how many humans we have in Nigeria.

Aesop's Fable
The Mule

A mule had grown fat and wanton from his huge daily rations of corn, and one day, as he was jumping, kicking and gamboling about the fields, he thought to himself, "My mother must surely have been a thoroughbred racer, and I'm quite as good as she ever was!"

But he was soon exhausted from the galloping and frisking, and all at once he remembered that his sire had been nothing but an ass.

(We may pretend that we are human, but our actions will always tell otherwise).

5. *How Many Are We Really in Nigeria?* [2]

I began what some may say amounts to an outrageous discourse on how many we really are in Nigeria. By how many I was referring to the real humans who constitute the national population and who must, of necessity, be separated from the millions of the other beings that walk the land, erect, human-like. I brought out three key issues that my readers may have to examine very closely. One is that my quarrel is not with the official population estimate published by the National Population Commission (NPC)–a figure I have no quarrel with because of its irrelevance to the issue at hand. Second, is that this official estimate is fictive, fraudulent and absurd as it does not, on the basis of any known demographic or statistical evaluation, approximate the number of beings in the country. Third, and most painful and tragic is the conclusion I reached, reluctantly, that two categories of beings make up the Nigerian population: a few number of humans who live in the country, and whose population may be in the low millions, and the mass of beings who also dwell in the land, animalized, bestialized, and most annoyingly, have accepted their sub-human condition which they regurgitate out on a daily basis.

On closer examination, it became instantly clear to me, instinctually, intellectually and with the force of social epiphany which conditions draw human consciousness, that this is a subject that one can accuse me of being obsessed with. The second and third essays I penned on commencing this column–"Our National Zombie Ethic" and "Combating the Zombie Mentality" are comfortably situated within the matrix of the present exploration. Zombies are walking, ritually re-animated corpses, who are only human in form and shape but whose soul, unreflective mentality, attitude and blind, uncritical social existence are shorn of all known human traits.

It is precisely the full understanding of this in-humanity or lack of humanness that attracted tragic consequences for the late Afro-Jazz star, Fela Anikulapo-Kuti, at the hands of those he defined by this necrophilic phenomenon. And if my conclusion in the two essays is that the Zombie syndrome explains much that is in the life of very many Nigerians, the logical conclusion is that those millions of Zombies that we see everyday and count as our friends, work-mates and business associates are not humans after all. The logic of Zombism thus explains the non-humanness of millions of Nigerians in a fused dialectic of identity, accommodation, behavioural pattern and mindset.

It is quite possible that someone can accuse me of insufferable arrogance, of being intolerant, extremist and condescending in my views. Others may even charge that I am also tarred with the same brush of Zombism and sub-humanness. Yet, there will be those who will be very quick to explain away this odious and paralytic national condition with the theory of alienation. They will try to situate this socio-psychological phenomenon within the context of national underdevelopment and mass pauperization of the people, and as an extreme indication of the illogic of capitalist oppression and dehumanization of whole entities. They will allude to the collapse of the middle class with its attendant economic, social and moral consequences, and the rising unemployment and layoffs among the young and the middle-aged. They will also point at the steady buccaneering of the national wealth in the hands of a tiny segment of a bloated, flatulent parasitic class and the attendant emergence of the culture of groveling, timidity, irrationality and wanton subservience by the mass of the people who, being thoroughly alienated, express their social presence in the form of the sordid and reprehensible social consciousness and reality I am unfairly attacking.

I don't buy any of this argument. The very fact that I understand this situation very well and I am intent on exposing it means that I have already embarked on the process of reclaiming my own diminished humanity. I have decided to say no to my non-human existence, my moment of unbecoming, indeed my nothingness. Others are called upon to do so, so that collectively, a coordinate outrage can be unleashed against this altar of national imbecility empowered by the ritual of mass denial, mass inexistence and worship of social idiocy.

Again, no theory can explain a situation that has become peculiarly Nigerian in all its solemn declarations and testaments. Not the theory of alienation or the theory of the forms of false consciousness engendered by national diversities – the key weapons the ruling elite have been accused of using to hold the people down, to trample on their humanity, their life-force, and their essence as a people. Nigerians can borrow a leaf from the "red" and "blue" shirt of Thailand – a people no less impoverished and bestialized by their elite and no more educated and socially consciousness than the average Nigerian. They should borrow a leaf from the Egyptians, Moroccans, Tunisians and Algerians who are prepared to shoot down their government because of a marginal increase in the price of bread, and not ask their househelp why she failed to buy the one made with cassava. By not demanding why they can no longer afford semovita and have rather settled for eba, elubo, or rogo, they have severed the umbilicus that binds beings to their humanness and have already crossed the threshold of unreason and into the realm of animal-like irrationality. They have nobody to blame, not the elite and not an amorphous system they have accepted as real and authentic.

These days, I have drastically limited my movement around Abuja in my car. Though I can ill-afford the exorbitant taxi charges, day in, day out, I have reluctantly decided that it will be my only means of transportation from Monday to Friday. I am now a weekend driver when the roads are free from the raging storm of madness, sheer lunacy and irrationality that define road use. Even in the taxi, I will have my eyes permanently shut, expecting to hear crunching and ripping metal sound as cars slam into one another.

Road junctions, on well tarred roads, and even with traffic light or road wardens at work, are littered with smashed up vehicles, broken limbs, human blood. If you take a drive or are driven along Ahmadu Bello Way, Mohammed Buhari Way, Aminu Kano Crescent, Nnamdi Azikiwe Expressway, Sani Abacha Expressway or any of the major road arteries in the cities, what you see defies description. Vehicles tear at one another in a haphazard manner, crossing lanes, re-crossing them and surging in various directions in a mindless fashion. You will not see the poetry of road usage or its symmetry, of decency, of regularity and rational conduct. 90% of the road users appear unsure of what they are out there doing, permanently confused, bemused. How can anyone convince me that the road users are human beings, and should be counted as part of the Nigerian human population?

Or rather take a drive to a petrol station at the height of fuel scarcity and have your sight and other senses assailed by the sordid display of beastly conducts. Apart from the social atrocity in beings queuing for over 72hrs for fuel, patiently and apparently without a care in the world (remember that I have already classified them as Zombies), you will also witness clenched fists pounding one another at the station entrances, hooting of horns, use of expletives, dragging, scuffles, and what have you.

Maybe you too can begin to agree with me that it is difficult to ascertain how many we really are in Nigeria.

Aesop's Fable
The Eagle and the Arrow

A bowman took aim at an eagle and struck him in the heart. As the eagle turned his head in the agony of death, he saw that the arrow was winged with his own feathers. "How sharper and more painful," said he, "are the wounds made by weapons we ourselves have supplied."

(We Nigerians constantly supply the oppressors with the weapons to continue our dehumanization and imbecilization.)

6. *The Illogic of Revenue Allocation*

We have a naïve penchant of believing all that we read in the dailies (including the present piece). Our naivety is impressionably child-like, ever trusting the newspapers to tell the truth always, in our hopes and expectations that our journalists and opinion page commentators are infallible. Because we don't usually subject the concepts, notions and terms that define national discourse and public policy space to close analytic examination we have steadily foisted on ourselves a "believe" ethic that is harmful to critical thought. We plod along, complacent in our shared wisdom and unalarmed that often times, we are merely swallowing prejudices, half truths, and distorted information and downright falsehood as a gospel or Koranic truth.

The other day, a friend was visibly angry about the games President Yar'adua and his close aides were playing on the nation given the false sightings that characterize his imminent appearance. His grouse was that he wasted four whole hours at the National Mosque waiting for Mr President to appear when he would have been at his favourite garden eating grilled fresh fish. When I asked him why he thought President Yar'adua would attend that particular jummat prayer, he asked me, almost rudely, whether I didn't hear that he was scheduled to attend the service, and if I did not know that thousands of people, including important dignitaries, and foreign and local journalists, were all there because it was said he would appear without fail.

When I reminded him that his information must have come from a *Next* newspaper news item, he waved that away as being unimportant, insisting rather harshly that we have all been taken for a ride. It is amazing the plain gullibility of Nigerians when it comes to what they read in the newspapers. My friend is apparently unconcerned about the channel of official presidential communication in such matters. He was unimpressed that no presidential spokesperson put out such information; neither did the *Next* report quote any single verifiable source in its story beyond the usual nonsense about usually reliable sources or some such *bla bla*.

Even worse is the situation at the public policy concept level where Nigerians are taken for a ride on a constant basis. Because our mass media have bought into this indolent tradition, they end up spewing out all manners of official policy illogicalities as if they are tested facts. Take the issue of taxpayers money, which is being used as a basis of compelling governments to deliver certain services, without which they would be adjusted as having failed in their obligations to society. We constantly hear people moaning about the misuse of taxpayers money, the waste of tax-payers money and the massive theft of taxpayers money. You begin to wonder, what tax and what payer. Has anybody taken pains to analyze the percentage of taxpayers money in the national GDP or its constituent part in, say, the 2010 budget? The notion of taxpayers' money is an errant absurdity, a pernicious falsehood that gives all of us an air of unearned importance and the shaky moral foundation on which to thunder abuse at those who misgovern us.

To demand that government should use taxpayers money wisely and judiciously is a blatant fallacy, because the money that comes from individual and even corporate tax is an infinitesimal percentage of the national revenue base. More horrendous is the new tax regime the state governments have devised to increase their internally generated revenue portfolio because it does nothing but impoverish a people already bestialized by penury, while adding little or nothing to such a state's utilizable revenue. Possible exceptions to this are Lagos, Kano, Rivers, and a few other states because of their very special circumstances.

The most ridiculous of this falsehood, purchased and swallowed wholesale by the public, is the notion of Revenue Allocation. This revolting term has gone unchallenged for God knows how long, recycled by all successive regimes, and dished out to an unsuspecting public by the mass media. The monthly sordid ritual of sharing money between the three governmental tiers are reported diligently in the mass media without commentary, but just as a given, natural, normal, ordinary fact of life. The same goes for the periodic sharing of the revenue in the "excess crude amount" by all the tiers of the government.

Has just about anybody paused to ponder about the implication of 36 people gathering in Abuja every month with, maybe, bulky briefcases, and then just going away after sharing money. Has anybody wondered about what is being shared and the implication of this is to the concept of fiscal federalism?

Again, has anybody spared a thought about the total disconnection between people and their wealth, the distance such a practice creates between the rulers and the led, and if in fact governance is not merely an act of benevolence?

Take, for example, a state whose internally generated revenue is but one percent of its monthly ₦5bn allocation. Assuming, for example, God forbid, such a state is to witness a combination of tsunami, earthquake, tornado and hurricane that flatten its farmlands and businesses to the ground and even finish off all its population minus the Governor, his Accountant-General and his Commissioner for Finance. What difference does these natural disasters and loss of its "productive" population make to what that state will collect at the next allocation meeting? Nothing! It will still cart away its ₦5bn less one percent back home to its denuded and depopulated land.

A friend of mine wondered aloud one day why his state governor has not yet remembered to call on his services despite his impressive credentials, uncommon talent, sense of industry and enterprise and acute and piercing intellect. I was quick to remind him that no governor will ever require his services because he won't be adding value to governance. The governor has all the money he needs from the monthly allocation. If he has any shortfall, he and his colleagues will apply excruciating pressure on the president to share part of the excess crude money. I also reminded him that his governor will only seek him out if there is a yawning gulf between what he intends to achieve and the money available to him to do so. If a governor has an annual developmental target of, say ₦10bn and can only find ₦5bn, no matter how hard he tries, he must look for help. He will call on the services of the best and the brightest to help him bridge the gap. Very few governors have such a challenge, so why would my friend hope to be drafted for service when the governor's goons, errand boys, shoe shiners and lackeys are very much available to be made Commissioners, Special Advisers and Chairmen and Members of important Corporations.

Taxpayers don't hire governments in Nigeria, oil does. Loyalty is to oil and the wealth it generates. We all recall the last American Presidential election during which both Obama and McCain repeatedly told the American people what they will do for them if they are hired for the job. The operative term is hired for the job, because national revenue should consist of the aggregate of individual and corporation taxes pulled together as collective national wealth. This wealth will be put in the care of someone, with deep trust, to use it well for the common good.

I may be wrong but the horror of sharing money every month may indeed be another uniquely Nigerian experience, spectacle and phenomenon. This nightmare scenario will continue to endure until oil ceases to hire our government. One way to end this charade is to ask God to dry up all the oil wells in Nigeria overnight, so that we will really know who is who. If this measure appears extreme, then let the National Assembly enact a law that will place all our oil revenue into an untouchable, out of reach escrow account for 10 years. This will be a good starting point.

Aesop's Fable
The Moon and Her Mother

The Moon once asked her mother to make her a little cloak that would fit her well.

"How can I make a cloak to fit you?" her mother asked. "Right now you're a new moon, but soon you'll turn into a half moon, and later you'll become neither one nor the other."

(In Nigeria, with regard to public policy concepts, it's the more you look, the less you see.)

RECOMMENDED BOOKS AND OTHER RESEARCH MATERIALS FOR FURTHER READING

Adetula, Victor A. O. ed. *Money and Politics in Nigeria*. Abuja: IFES-Nigeria, 2008.

Africa Peace Review (Journal of Centre for Peace Research and Conflict Resolution, National Defence College Abuja, Nigeria). *Survey of Conflicts in Nigeria*, 2003.

Agbagha, Mma. *Pressure Group Politics*. Ibadan: Spectrum Books, 2003.

Agbaje, Adigun A.B. ed. *Nigeria's Struggle for Democracy and Good Governance*. Ibadan: University of Ibadan Press, 2004.

Albert, Isaac Olawale. ed. *Perspectives on Peace and Conflict in Africa*. Ibadan: John Archers Publishers, 2005.

———————— *et al*. *Perspectives on the 2003 Elections in Nigeria*. Abuja/Ibadan: IDASA-NIGERIA/Stirling-Horden Publishers, 2007.

———————— & Derrick Marco. ed. *Animus and Apologia: Campaign Advertorials and the Gamble for Power in the 2003 and 2007 Elections in Nigeria*. Abuja/Ibadan: IDASA-NIGERIA/Stirling-Horden Publishers, 2007.

Alele-Williams, Grace. *Women and Gender Equality for a Better Society in Nigeria*. Lagos: Leaven Club International, 2002.

Alkali, M. N. ed. *Nigeria in the Transition Years (1993-1999)*. Presidential Advisory Committee/NIPPS, 1999.

Alozieuwa, Simeon H.O. *From Parliamentarism to Militocracy and Presidentialism: Nigeria in Quest for Stable Political*

Order. Abuja: Authentic Media Networks, 2008.

Alubo, Ogoh. *Ethnic and Citizenship Crises in the Central Region Nigeria.* Ibadan: PEFS University of Ibadan/Eddy Asae Nigeria Press, 2006.

Arowolo, Dare E. & Olukemi A. Aluko. "Democracy, Political Participation and Good Governance in Nigeria". *International Journal of Development and Sustainability,* Volume 1, Number 3, 2012, pp. 797-809.

Azar, Edwards. *The Management of Protracted Conflict: Theory and Cases.* Dartmouth: Aldershot, 1990.

Best, Shedrack Gaya. ed. *Introduction to Peace and Conflict Studies in West Africa: A Reader.* Ibadan: Spectrum Books, nd.

Burton, John. *Conflict Resolution and Prevention.* St. Martin Press, 1990.

Chua, Amy. *World on Fire: How Exporting Free Market Democracy Breeds Ethnic Hatred and Global Instability.* London: Arrow Books, 2003.

Ego-Alowes, Jimanze. *Minorities as Competitive Overlords.* Lagos: The Stone Press, 2013.

Fagbemi, Ayokunle *et al. Conflict Monitoring in Nigeria: Developing Civil Society Action for Early Warning and Early Response.* Lagos: WANEP, 2004.

Golwa, Joseph H. P. & Ochinya O. Ojiji. ed. *Dialogue on Citizenship in Nigeria.* Abuja: IPCR, 2008.

Gurr, Ted and B. Harff. *Ethnic Conflict in World Politics.* San Francisco: West View Press, 1994.

Harnischfeger, Johannes. *Democratization and Islamic Law: The Sharia Conflict in Nigeria.* Frankfurt/New York: Campus Verlag, 2008.

Ibrahim, Jibrin. compl & ed. *Nigeria Elections 2007: Defending the People's Mandate.* Abuja: Global Rights, 2005.

Ihonvbere, Julius O. *Nigeria: The Politics of Adjustment and Democracy.* Transaction Publishers, 1994.

Imobighe, Thomas, A. *Civil Society and Ethnic Conflict Management in Nigeria.* Ibadan: Spectrum Books, 2003.

————————— *et al. Conflict and Instability in The Niger*

Delta: The Warri Case. Ibadan: Spectrum Books, 2002.

IPCR. *Strategic Conflict Assessment of Nigeria: Consolidated and Zonal Reports, 2003.*

Irobi, Emmy Godwin. "Ethnic Conflict Management in Africa: A Comparative Case Study of Nigeria and South Africa", *Intractability*, University of Colorado, May 2005.

Jega, Attahiru. *Democracy, Good Governance and Development in Nigeria*. Ibadan: Spectrum Books, 2007.

Kukah, Matthew Hassan. *Democracy and Civil Society in Nigeria*. Ibadan: Spectrum Books, 2002.

Marco, Derrick. ed. *Conflict Tracking Dossiers*. Abuja: IDASA-NIGERIA, 2007.

MCIA. Occasional Papers. "MCIA and Elections, Good Governance and Peace Building in Africa: A Compendium of Reports". MCIA, 2006.

Mustapha, Abdul Raufu. "Civil Rights and Pro-democracy Groups in and outside Nigeria". Institut Francais de Recherche en Afrique, Open Edition, 2001, pp. 145-183.

Nkire, Sam. *The Nigeria Story.* Abuja: Niger Press Ltd, 2008.

Nnoli, Okwudiba. *Ethnic Politics in Nigeria*. Enugu: Fourth Dimension Publishers, 1980.

———————— ed. *Communal Conflict and Population Displacement in Nigeria*. Enugu: SNAAP Press, 2003.

Nwankwo, Arthur Agwuncha. *Nigeria: The Political Transition and the Future of Democracy.* Enugu: Fourth Dimension Publishers, 1993.

Nwankwo, Clement & Olayinka Lawal. ed. *Legislative Agenda for Legal Reforms and Human Rights*. Constitutional Rights Project (CRP), 2002.

Obi, Amanze. *Delicate Distress: An Interpreter's Account of the Nigerian Dilemma.* Ibadan: Stirling-Horden Publishers, 2013.

Ogbonnia, Chiedozie Alex. *Banana Peel: The Burden of Legislature in Nigeria.* Enugu: CIDJAP, 2009.

Oko, Okechukwu. *Key Problems for Democracy in Nigeria.* London: Edwin Mellen, 2010.

Olufemi, Fatile Jacob. "The Role of Civil Society

Organizations in Conflict Management in Nigeria", Asian Economic and Social Society's International *Journal of Asian Social Science*, Vol. 2, Issue5, May 2012, pp. 720-729.

Osaghae, Eghosa E. "Managing Multiple Minority Problems in a Divided Society: The Nigerian Experience", *The Journal of Modern African Studies*, Vol. 36, No. 1, 1998, pp. 1-24.

Oshita Oshita. *Conflict Management in Nigeria: Issues and Challenges*. London: Adonis & Abbey Publishers, 2007.

Otite, Onigu. *Ethnic Pluralism, Ethnicity and Ethnic Conflicts in Nigeria*. Ibadan: Shaneson Ltd, 1990, 2000.

———————— & Isaac Olawale Albert. ed. *Community Conflicts in Nigeria: Management, Resolution and Transformation*. Ibadan: Spectrum Books, 1999, 2001.

Paden, John N. *Postelection Conflict Management in Nigeria: The Challenges of National Unity*. Washington, DC: George Mason University Press, 2013.

———————— *Muslim Civic Cultures and Conflict Resolution: The Challenge of Democratic Federalism in Nigeria*. Washington, DC: Brookings Institution Press, 2005.

Society for Peace Studies. *Peace Studies and Practice* (Journal), Vol. 1, No. 1, June, 2006.

Suberu, Rotimi. *Federalism and Ethnic Conflict in Nigeria*. Washington, DC: USIP, 2001.

———————— *Ethnic Minority Conflicts and Governance in Nigeria*. Ibadan: Spectrum Books, 1996.

Toure, Kazah Toure. *Ethno-Religious Conflicts in Kaduna State*. Kaduna: Human Rights Monitor, 2003.

Transition Monitoring Group. "Do the Votes Count? Final Report of the 2003 General Elections in Nigeria". TMG. 2003.

www.ingramcontent.com/pod-product-compliance
Lightning Source LLC
Chambersburg PA
CBHW022310280326
41932CB00010B/1052